PAIGNTON

AFTER THE *Railway Came*

THE STORY OF THE DEVELOPMENT OF PAIGNTON
1859 - MID 1960's

Enjoy!

Harold Rumbelow

BY W. HAROLD RUMBELOW FRICS

First Published in Great Britain in 2005 by
W. Harold Rumbelow

ISBN 0-9546071-1-2

Design and production
Creative Media Ltd, 35 Woodland Park, Paignton, TQ3 2ST
www.mhcreativemedia.co.uk

Printed and bound by Antony Rowe Ltd, Eastbourne

CONTENTS

The Author

William Harold Rumbelow (generally known as Harold) was born on the 28th February 1911 at No. 3 Gasworks Cottages, Cecil Road, Paignton (long since demolished). He has lived in Paignton since birth.

He attended Polsham Road Infants School at the age of three and was transferred to Curledge Street Boys School at the age of seven or eight.

In 1922 he obtained a scholarship to the Torquay Secondary School for Boys (later to become the Torquay Boys Grammar School) which at that time was part fee paying.

In 1927 he left school, having passed the Cambridge School Certificate Examination.

In September 1927 he became an articled pupil Quantity Surveyor with Messrs Harris and Hills at No. 36 Hyde Road, Paignton (now No. 46). The Articles were for four years and his father paid a premium of £100 which was returnable on completion of the Articles.

He qualified as a Professional Associate of the Chartered Surveyors Institution (later the RICS) in 1933 and became a Fellow in 1946.

Following the outbreak of war in 1939, the firm of W T Hills was appointed by the War Office as Resident Surveyors for a large Army Supply Reserve Depot at Norton Fitzwarren on the outskirts of Taunton. A condition of the appointment was that an office be set up on site in charge of a senior surveyor. On the 1st January 1940 Harold moved into "digs" in Taunton and set up an office in a large timber building on site, and built up a staff of five. It was a very large contract, on an open field site, involving the construction of road and rail transport sheds. The site office was maintained until the end of the war.

In about 1941 Hills were appointed by the Air Ministry for a new RAF Station to be constructed at Chilbolton near Andover. This entailed setting up another site office with staff and this was run by Harold in conjunction with the Taunton contract and involved frequent visits to the site. Harold stayed with a family in Taunton from Mondays to Thursdays returning to contact the Torquay office.

During weekends he served with the local Home Guard Platoon doing

training and guard duties at the old Goodrington Hotel.

He became a Partner in W T Hills & Co., Chartered Quantity Surveyors in 1941 and retired as Senior Partner in 1973.

His main recreation has been an interest in sailing; built his first sailing dinghy and joined The Torbay Sailing Club (later Paignton Sailing Club) in 1936 and was elected as its first Honorary Admiral for life in 1985 on retiring as Honorary Secretary after many years and having served as a Flag Officer.

He married in 1935, became a widower in 2001 and has a family of a son and daughter, five grandchildren and eleven great grandchildren.

An Appreciation

The author is indebted to Mr A C (Charles) Easterbrook, a Paigntonian "born and bred" and Mr Tony Moss, Chairman of the Paignton Preservation and Local History Society who undertook the task of editing, amending and amplifying the original draft. To Mr Anthony Procter for information on his family and building developments, and to members of various organisations who have provided me with details of their early history. Thanks also due to Kay Rumbelow, my daughter-in-law, who turned my original illegible script into readable copy.

An apology

The author apologises for the fact that some of the information contained herein may be erroneous. Much of the text has been gathered from work written by others, but every effort has been made to check its veracity. Many readers may be better informed.
W.H.R.

Acknowledgements

The following works are the sources from which I have gathered the information to put together this book.

The History of Paignton - C.H. Patterson
Paignton Seven Reigns – Ralph Penwill
Pictures of Paignton – Peter Tully
Robinsons Directory of Paignton
The Torbay Towns – Anne Born
The Book of Paignton – Frank Pearce
Paignton & Its Attractions 1885 –
    The Devon County Standard
Chimps. Champs. And Elephants – Jack Baker
A History of W T Hills & Co. 1895-1989
Minutes & Records of Paignton Sailing Club

Contributions to "St Margaret's" Magazine
"Bygones" in the Herald Express
The Torbay Book – Chips Barber
Paignton, Torbay – John R. Pike
The Making of a Modern Resort –
    Henry J. Lethbridge

Foreword

This is not meant to be an historical work and does not include any photographs. It is an analysis of what has been written by others, showing the development of all the different sections of the community, presented chronologically, to illustrate the remarkable transformation of Paignton following the coming of the railway.

The period under review has been limited to end in the middle 1960's as, in the author's opinion, development became re-development and demolition started to take over from construction.

Very little has been written about the "war years" as development, generally, was halted during this period.

Note: Any money accruing to the author arising from the publication of this book will be donated to the Devon Air Ambulance Trust.

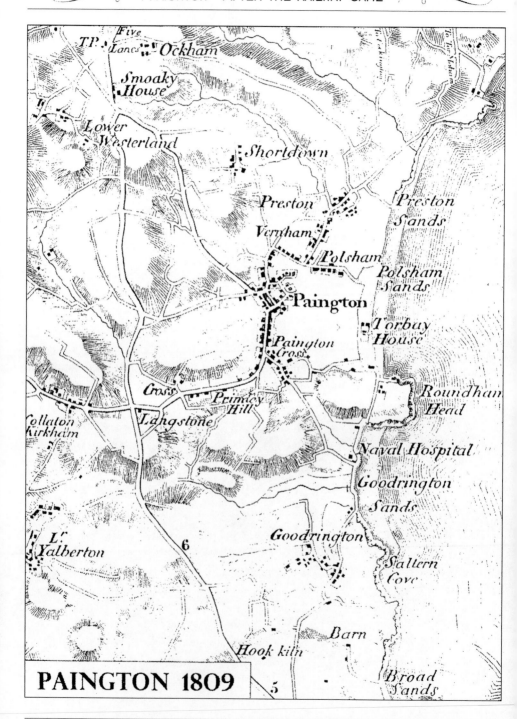

Five Lanes
T.P.
Ockham
Smoaky House
Lower Westerland
Shortdown
Preston
Vernham
Preston Sands
Polsham
Polsham Sands
Paington
Torbay House
Paington Cross
Cross
Primley Hill
Langstone
Collaton Kirkham
Roundham Head
Naval Hospital
Goodrington Sands
Goodrington
Saltern Cove
L.r Yalberton
6
Barn
Hook kiln
Broad Sands

PAINGTON 1809

5

CHAPTER ONE

Paignton as it Was

IN THE LATE 1850's PAIGNTON WAS A SMALL town with a population of about 3000. It was centred around the Parish Church, the remains of the old Bishops Palace and the main water supply. It was also the spot where the road from Cockington and Torre divided into two, one to Totnes and the other to Kingswear (for Dartmouth and Brixham).

It was largely an agricultural district depending on the surrounding orchards, the renowned "flatpole" cabbages and a small fishing community around the harbour.

There was practically nothing to the east of the main road except marshland and reed beds and the elevated area of Roundham Head where the cabbages were grown. Beyond the marshland were large sand dunes along the sea shore. Preston was undeveloped farmland.

The main street was Winner Street which connected the Church Street area with the main road to Totnes.
Rough roads connected the main road to the sea front area and the harbour, such as Polsham Road, Fisher Street and Sands Road.

There was a large area of land to the south of the old Bishops Palace and east of Winner Street which was once a deer park and was used for the growing of vegetables. This was to become Palace Avenue.

There were three non-conformist chapels and a small school in Church Street. There were at least twelve public houses or inns!

The land in and around the town was in the hands of a few families, the Belfields (probably the largest) the Butlands, Distins, Hunts, Jacksons and Goodridges.

Most of the land behind the foreshore was owned by Mr McLean.

CHAPTER TWO

The Developers

THE ENTREPRENEURS

Mr McLean

A Mr McLean owned a large area of land adjacent to the Paignton foreshore, including Torbay House. In 1866 he sold by auction 200 acres of this land and in May 1866 he conveyed Polsham Green to the town on condition that the Local Board would in future check all sea encroachments.

Mr R Fletcher

Mr Fletcher was a solicitor and property developer from Birmingham. In 1865 he bought Torbay House and 60 acres of land adjoining the shore and beach. With the aid of Mr G S Bridgman (referred to later) he produced plans for the future extension of Paignton seaward. This greatly enhanced the value of contiguous building land. He died intestate in 1877 and his Trustees handed over Paignton Green South to the Local Board.

Mr Arthur Hyde Dendy

Arthur Hyde Dendy was born in London in 1821, but practised as a solicitor in Birmingham. He lived for a time in Torquay before coming to Paignton. He was responsible for much of the early development of Paignton as more fully described in later chapters. One of his earliest projects was the purchase of land on the Steartfield Estate which included Parkfield House, where he lived between 1878 and 1879. His largest undertakings were Paignton Pier, the Gerston Hotel and the Bijou Theatre. He died on August 13th, 1886.

Mr William Lambshead

William Lambshead was a member of an Ipplepen family, born in 1848. He came to Paignton in his twenties to manage Dellers Grocery Store in Winner Street. He married Mr Deller's eldest daughter Elizabeth Anne and eventually took over the business, but retained the name Dellers.

He was part of a consortium which developed Palace Avenue where he opened Dellers Stores. He built Queens Park Mansions and Dellers Café. He was Chairman of the Local Board from 1873 to 1877. He died in March 1932.

Mr Henry John Bailey

Not much is know of his personal life. He built Tower House in Fisher Street in 1890 and also built Coniston House in Sands Road. He built Baileys Hotel in Station Square and Baileys Emporium in Winner Street. All his buildings bear a marked resemblance in the use of limestone and Bathstone.

The Singer Family

Isaac Merritt Singer was born in New York State USA in 1811. He married at the age of 19 and at the age of 21 was the father of two children. He married a second time and had ten children. In 1863 he married Isabella Eugene Summerville by whom he had six children.

In America he had assisted in the development of a sewing machine for mass production and by 1860 The Singer Sewing Machine Company was the largest producer of sewing machines in America and Europe.

He came to England in 1870 and bought the Fernham Estate in 1871. He later commissioned George Sowdon Bridgman to design the first mansion known as "The Wigwam". He died on 23rd July 1875.

The eldest son was Adrian Mortimer Singer, born in New York in 1863 and came to live with the family at Oldway. He spent much of his time sailing, was made a K.B.E. in 1920 after which he was known locally as Sir Mortimer Singer.

He presented the Choir Vestries to the Parish Church.

He died in 1929.

The second son was Washington Grant Merritt Singer, born in 1866 on the liner "Great Eastern" crossing the Atlantic. He built the Merritt Flats in St. Michaels. He died in 1934.

The third son was Paris Eugene Singer, born in 1867 and who lived for many years at Oldway. He made many alterations and commissioned the architect G S Bridgman to design Oldway Mansion which was completed in 1907. He was responsible for much of the development of Preston as a residential area. He was involved with Isadora Duncan by whom he had two children. He presented the organ to the Parish Church.

The Primley Estate – The Belfields and Whitleys

For many years Primley House had been occupied by the Belfield family who owned about one third of the land in and around Paignton. John F Belfield was Chairman of the local Board of Health in 1863.

In 1898 Edward Whitley, a prosperous brewer living in Liverpool, died suddenly leaving his widow, Mrs Eleanor Whitley and five children.

Mrs Whitley decided to move to Devon. She purchased the Primley Estate and the family moved to Primley House in 1904.

Eventually, two sons, William and Herbert, took over the running of the estate and formed the W & H Whitely Partnership developing the agricultural and stockbreeding branch of the estate, William, was interested in the agricultural side and in birds and wildlife.

Eventually William broke away from the partnership to concentrate on farming at Buckland in the Moor, on the southern edge of Dartmoor, whilst Herbert concentrated on his animals and plants and the start of what was to become Primley Zoo, as dealt with in Chapter 28.

In about 1908 the Whitley brothers appointed Mr Fred E Bowen as estate agent and secretary and it was Mr Bowen who was responsible for the development of large areas of the estate into residential districts such as Cliff Road, Osney Crescent and the Clennon area.

Mr Herbert Whitley died in 1955 and shortly after his death the Herbert Whitley Trust was established under the control of Mr Whitley's friend of many years, Mr Philip Michelmore.

THE ARCHITECTS

George Sowdon Bridgman

G S Bridgman is often known as "The Father of Paignton". He was born in 1839 and spent his early life in Torquay, spent some time in London, but returned in 1854 to serve articles with a local builder.

He qualified in 1860 and set up his own practice. He designed numerous buildings and developments in the area, almost too numerous to mention. Some of his chief works in Paignton include; Oldway Mansion, the sea wall on Paignton Seafront, Paignton Pier, the lay out of Paignton Green and Victoria Park. He collaborated in the design and layout of Palace Avenue and the Public Hall.

After some time in Paignton he moved to Torquay in January 1902 where he stayed until his death in April 1925 at the age of 86.

Some years earlier he had taken his son Norman into partnership and the practice became know at Bridgman & Bridgman.

In due course Norman's son, Gerald, qualified and joined the practice. For many years the office was above the shops on the corner of Palace Avenue and Bishops Place.

The practice closed when Gerald Bridgman emigrated to South Africa.

W G Couldrey

Walter George Couldrey set up practice in Paignton in the 1880's. In November of that year he prepared the plans for the new Cemetery and Chapel.

In 1886 be collaborated with a London architect Edward Gabriel in the design of Christ Church. Also in 1886 he joined Mr Washington Singer, G S Bridgman and Mr Bartlett in the development of Palace Avenue. It is known that he designed the buildings on the west side of Palace Avenue and he was also responsible for the layout of the Adelphi Road area where he later lived for a time.

He occupied offices in Palace Avenue on the first floor of the building on the corner of Palace Avenue and Coverdale Road (later Church's China Shop). He designed the original cemetery and chapel.

He later took his son Norman into partnership (locally known as Major Couldrey) using the title W G Couldrey & Son. The firm were the architects for the rebuilding of the old Commercial Hotel in Dartmouth Road (destroyed by fire) and known as "The Coverdale". He died in December 1950.

Hyams and Hobgen

Not much is known about the firm which had offices in Palace Avenue. They were the architects for Dellers Café and The Picture House.

Other Architects

Architects who played a large part in the later development of Paignton were Graham Colborne who had an office in Hyde Road, Ernest Ladbury, who had an office in Victoria Street and C F J Thurley who designed the Festival Theatre. Later many more practices opened up.

THE SURVEYORS

More directly concerned with buildings rather than land are Quantity Surveyors. Until recent years many people had not heard of Quantity Surveyors so perhaps a little information might help (if slightly personally biased!)

Quantity Surveyors may be said "to hold the purse strings" of building projects. They work in close liaison with architects in preparing preliminary estimates of the likely cost, preparing Bills of Quantities and in some cases specifications, for the invitation of tenders; checking, pricing and advising on tenders; preparing valuations for the interim payments to contractors and finally preparing and agreeing the final cost with the contractor. They are often engaged in settling building disputes. In 1906 local builders decided they would not tender for

work over £100 without Bills of Quantities and in May 1913 decided not to tender for work over £150 without Bills of Quantities.

Vincent Cattermole Brown

Vincent Cattermole Brown was born in London in 1854. At the age of 21 he gave his occupation as a surveyor's clerk. He moved to Paignton in the mid 1880's when he became associated with the architect W G Couldrey.

A London architect, Edward Gabriel, collaborated with W G Couldrey on the design of Christ Church and the specification dated 1886 bears both their names and it is thought that this association brought Brown and Couldrey closer together. He later went into partnership with Richard Harris, a builder with a yard in Hyde Road, who had been the foreman in charge of the construction of Paignton Pier.

After several years he set up practice on his own and in Kelly's Directory of 1897 he is described as a surveyor, practising at No 56 Victoria Street (on the corner of Gerston Road, built in 1893). There is evidence that he continued to work in close co-operation with W G Couldrey.

In the period 1905-1907 he prepared Bills of Quantities for Messrs Purvis & Purvis, a firm of consulting engineers of Exeter and Edinburgh and in association with that firm prepared the Bills of Quantities for the Electric Light Station for the Paignton Electric Light & Power Company.

Further Bills of Quantities were prepared in conjunction with W G Couldrey.

Owing to ill health he closed his office in Victoria Street and in 1910 he was practising as a Quantity Surveyor from his home address "Carisbrooke" Adelphi Road, very near the residence of W G Couldrey. He died in June 1912.

George Sealley Harris

Born in 1876 the son of Richard Harris, the builder in Hyde Road, George Harris started his career working for his father, keeping records, measuring and pricing building work and generally assisting in the office.

He joined V C Brown (see above) as an assistant in about 1900 and it was here that he was taught the basics of quantity surveying.

On V C Brown's decision to close his office in Victoria Street he took a room in his father's premises at No 36 Hyde Road (now No 46) helping V C Brown and gradually taking over his practice, and by 1911 was producing Bills of Quantities under his own name, one of the earliest being that for Torquay Pavilion which was started in July of that year.

No records are available of G S Harris' practice during the war years, 1914-1918, but it is thought that be continued in practice and did not see military service because he suffered deafness. He died in 1949.

William Thomas Hills

Early in 1920 G S Harris engaged an assistant, William Thomas Hills, who had been demobilised some months earlier.

W T Hills was born in Cambridgeshire in 1893. After leaving school he attended a technical college in London and then spent two years with a firm of builders in Cambridge attending evening classes in building construction and quantity surveying. After four years in the army he spent a few months with a quantity surveyor in Uxbridge before joining G S Harris in 1920. He qualified as a Professional Associate of the Surveyors Institution (now RICS) in 1922.

G S Harris took W T Hills into partnership in January 1923. The title of the firm became Harris & Hills practising from No 36 Hyde Road. The partnership flourished and was responsible for the Bills of Quantities for almost all building contracts in the area.

On 31st July 1931 the partnership was dissolved with two separate practices, G S Harris at Hyde Road, Paignton and W T Hills at 34 Fleet Street, Torquay.

W T Hills died in 1948 having taken William Harold Rumbelow into partnership in 1941.

In 1949 three former pupils of Harris & Hills, who had joined the separate firms, got together and formed a partnership of W T Hills & Co. They were W K Welton, C W E Drew and W H Rumbelow. Additional partners were incorporated as the firm expanded nationally. W K Welton and C W E Drew retired in 1970 and W H Rumbelow in 1973. Since then Harold Rumbelow's son Peter and more recently his grandson Philip have become directors in the limited company of Hills & Co, practising under the logo "Hills". Peter retired in August 2000.

THE SOLICITORS

The name of Eastley has been associated with the development of Paignton over many years. A Mr Flyde Eastley lived at Southview Manor, Southfield in about 1820. In Robinsons Directory of Paignton of 1851 the name of Forde Eastley appears as a solicitor residing at Kirkham House. Only one other solicitor is listed at the time. The name Eastley appears again in connection with the formation of The Public Hall Company in 1889 when the firm of Eastley, Jarman & Eastley are mentioned as joint company solicitors with Messrs Bartlett & Roberts.

The firm of Eastleys has always acted as agents for the Manor of Paignton and authorised

all leases and mortgages in the Paignton Town area. This duty extended to 1925. Eastleys office in Victoria Street has always been known as the Manor Office and the practice still exists today.

THE BUILDERS

Two builders are listed in Robinson's Directory of 1851, William Towell of Weston House and John Tozer of Culverhay Street. John Tozer built Redcliffe Tower.

Two firms of builders were involved in the early development of Paignton, Messrs C & R E Drew of Dartmouth Road and R Harris of Hyde Road.

Richard Harris had been employed by A H Dendy as foreman in charge of the building of Paignton Pier in 1878. He continued his association with Mr Dendy in the development of Hyde Road and Dendy Road. In 1891 a block of buildings was built on the corner of Hyde Road and what is now Dendy Road comprising a private house, builders office, a range of workshops, stables and yard and this became the premises of R Harris & Son, Builders. R Harris & Son built most of the houses in Hyde Road and Dendy Road and residences in other areas developed by Mr Dendy. The building business continued to a smaller degree until into the 1930's.

The firm of C & R E Drew consisted, in the early days, of two brothers who lived in Dartmouth Road and established offices and showrooms, an undertaking business and large workshops with access from the lane which ran at the west side rear of Dartmouth Road. They built many of the larger buildings such as Christ Church in 1886 and St Andrews Church in 1892. The firm also worked in close co-operation with the architect W J Couldrey and built several properties in Palace Avenue. They also built Dellers Café, Queens Park Mansions and Paignton Picture House.

The firm expanded and installed a saw mill and were the first firm to install woodworking machinery in their workshops.

The original founders were succeeded by generations of Drews.

Robinsons Directory lists the name of Charles Langler, Painter, Glazier and Paperhanger with premises in Culverhay Street (Higher Church Street). This is thought to be the founder of L A Langler & Sons, builders and decorators who established a business at 27 Winner Street. A photograph, taken outside the premises in 1906, shows a total of twenty-one employees and employers. The firm continued its business in Winner Street until well into the 1980's.

The name which will be remembered as a builder is that of Robert Ely (generally known as Bob) who, together with his son, was responsible for much of the development of

Preston. They built the Palladium Cinema (later demolished) in 1932.

Mr Rabbich was also involved in the building development of Preston, and he built Parkside Buildings off Torbay Road.

In the early 1930's the Procter family came to Paignton. Herbert Procter moved his family and building company lock, stock and barrel including a few loyal employees from Bradford in Yorkshire to Paignton. Herbert had been a developer and builder in the Bradford and Morecombe areas and he had owned the Morecombe Central Pier until it was destroyed by fire in 1933. Herbert initially rented a house in Morin Road, but later built a large residence on Barcombe Heights. He purchased land locally to build speculative houses (see Chapter Seven).

He had four sons; Arnold, Gordon, Maurice and Norman. Later Maurice and Norman returned to Yorkshire.

After the Second World War, Norman returned to Paignton and formed Clennon Developments Limited, and was responsible for building much of Wheatlands Road and Elsdale Road. The Company was subsequently taken over by his son Martin Procter.

The building company of J A Procter & Co. Ltd. was formed by Gordon and Arnold Procter who carried out extensive development and house building (see Chapter Seven).

Arnold Procter married Mona Cavanna, daughter of building contractor P D Cavanna in 1936. The Cavanna Company were also major developers in Paignton.

Between the World Wars and after World War Two many small building firms sprang up in the area and were chiefly employed in the building of houses in this rapidly expanding sphere.

CHAPTER THREE

Local Government

THE FIRST FORM OF LOCAL GOVERNMENT WAS THE LOCAL BOARD. Local Boards were provided under the Public Health Act 1848.

On July 28th 1863 Paignton adopted the Local Government Act 1858 and a meeting of the newly elected Local Board of Health was held at the Crown & Anchor Inn in Church Street on the 18th September 1863 under the Chairmanship of John F Belfield to consider the future development of the town. Meetings continued to be held at the Crown & Anchor Inn, but in April 1865 the Clerk, Mr Lidstone, offered a room in his house as an office for the Board to be open from 10 am to 3 pm. In December 1867 the Board decided to return to the Crown & Anchor Inn, but in December 1869 the meetings returned to Mr Lidstone's house.

Negotiations for the site of a Town Hall at the junction of New Street and Totnes Turnpike Road, between the Local Board and Mr Belfield of Primley House commenced in February 1867 and a lease from Mr Belfield was settled.

In June 1867 Mr Tarring was appointed Architect for the new building and in August of that year a tender of about £1900 by Messrs Bragg & Dyer was accepted. Difficulties over expenditure developed and work was suspended from September 1867 and work recommenced in 1869. The first meeting of the Board was in July 1870 when the officers; Clerk, Surveyor, Rates Officer, Water Superintendent and Inspector of Nuisances were installed. They had previously used their own residences as offices.

The Local Board met for the last time on December 29th 1894 and on December 31st 1894 the Paignton Urban District Council held its first meeting.

In June 1904 the County Court was requested to vacate the Town Hall as the whole of the premises were required for use by "the Council".

In October 1913 the Mill Yard Depot was considered to be too small and a site for a new depot in the old Well Street quarry was purchased from the Dendy Trustees and the new depot was completed at the end of 1914.

In 1922 Electric Light and Central Heating was installed in the Town Hall.

In the early years the Council officers using the Town Hall were The Town Clerk, Surveyor, Inspector of Nuisances and the Water Engineer.

In 1923 a storey was added to the Fire Station to accommodate the Public Health and Water Department.

In 1927 the Council staff comprised:

Clerk and Accountants' Department	**10**
Surveyors' Department	**10**
Public Health Isolation Hospital & Child Welfare	**10**
Collectors' Department	**3**
Water Department	**4**
Entertainment Department	**2**
Meteorologist (part time)	**1**
Pleasure Boat Inspector (part time)	**1**

Not all occupied space at the Town Hall. The Entertainment Department's office was a timber building at the rear of the Main Shelter on the Sea Front.

In May 1927 the Surveyors' Department moved to 5 Town Hall Terrace (23 Totnes Road). In October 1935 the Surveyors' Department needed extra space and took over the tenancy of the adjoining house, 25 Totnes Road. In February 1936 the Surveyors' Department Depot was moved from Well Street to a new site in Cecil Road.

In March 1937 the Collector moved from the Town Hall to 21 Totnes Road. The Public Health Department moved to 27 Totnes Road. Only the Clerk and Accountant were left in the Town Hall.

In January 1939 the Water Department moved from the Fire Station to 18 Midvale Road.

In 1940 the Chief Financial Officer (previously Accountant) moved from the Town Hall to 27 Totnes Road leaving the Clerk's Department as the only occupant.

Also in 1940 the Entertainment Department was moved from the Sea Front to 18 Totnes Road and the Waterworks Department moved from Midvale Road to "Westbrook" in Totnes Road.

In January 1945 the Treasurer retired and the policy of appointing a Bank Manager, which had been in operation since 1863, was revised and the Chief Financial officer was appointed Treasurer.

The first Parks Superintendent (Mr R Erskine) was appointed in March 1945.

During the war Oldway Mansion was requisitioned by the RAF, but in June 1945 application was made by the Council for a loan of £47,670 to purchase the 20 acre estate comprising the Mansion, Little Oldway and the Rotunda.

Oldway was purchased in September 1946 and at the time the second and third floors of the Mansion were divided into residential flats, all occupied. Temporary partitioning was erected in the reception rooms on the first floor to provide offices. The first department moved in on 39th September and the last on 18th November. The first Council Meeting at Oldway was held on 25th November 1946 and the official opening by Lady Leeds (grand daughter of Isaac Merritt Singer) on 18th December 1946.

In 1947 as flats became available, departments moved to the second and third floors. Possession of the last flat was obtained in December 1949.

During 1947 the Ballroom was improved and extended. Restoration of the grounds and gardens was completed in 1951. For a period, April 1948 to December 1950 the Rotunda was used by a film company, but the building has always been a problem to the Council.

The last Council meeting at the Town Hall was held in 28th October 1946.

Following the moves of most departments to Oldway in November 1946 a Rates Collection Office was established in the old Town Hall and the Entertainment Department, which had previously moved from 18 Totnes Road to 26 Hyde Road, also moved into the building.

As from October 1946 Town Planning powers were transferred from the Council to the South Devon Regional Planning Committee. In July 1948 the South Devon Regional Planning Committee was replaced by a Divisional Committee of the Devon County Council.

In November 1949 the town's coat of arms, together with the motto "Semper Acceptus" (Ever Welcome) received official approval.

An interesting development arising from the move to Oldway was the setting up of accommodation for the Registrar of Births, Deaths and Marriages and because of its surroundings Oldway became a popular venue for Registry Office weddings.

The first mention of a Registrar was recorded in Robinsons Directory of 1851 as being John Rossiter, Miller, Grocer and Earthenware Dealer in Winner Street. The office of Registrar remained in the Rossiter family for many years.

Following lengthy negotiations, Paignton Urban District Council ceased to exist and Paignton became part of the new County Borough of Torbay in 1968. An official photograph of the last gathering of the Paignton Urban District Council members and officers was taken at Oldway on 39th September 1967. The first mayor of the new County Borough was Mr A L Goodrich.

The County Borough was demoted to the Torbay Borough Council in 1974.

CHAPTER FOUR

Public Undertakings

GAS

Following a meeting of prospective shareholders in October 1859 the Paignton Gaslight Coal & Coke Company was formed in 1861 with a capital of £3,800, and the gas works built on a site between Mill Lane and Churchward Road.

Gas was first supplied in December 1860 and the first gas mains were laid in Winner Street and adjoining streets to provide street lighting with fishtail burners.

Gas supplies were slow to develop; one of the first areas to be supplied was Sands Road. By 1905 gas mains did not run beyond the then built-up area of the town.

By 1908 gas mains had been laid in Totnes Road as far as Collingwood Road, in Dartmouth Road as far as Fisher Street, and in Colley End as far as Quarry Terrace in Marldon Road.

In the early 1900's a row of six cottages were built on the boundary of the Gas Works fronting Cecil Road. These were subsequently demolished in about 1914 to allow for the expansion of the Gas Works, but the front walls were left standing with the window and door openings bricked up to serve as a boundary wall. The wall was subsequently demolished to allow for the widening of Cecil Road.

In the early days of the Gas Works the company had a small office inside the gateway at the junction of Mill Lane and Littlegate Road. This was where customers paid their bills and ordered supplies of coke, until offices and showrooms were opened in Palace Avenue in the position now occupied by Barclay's Bank.

Up to that time domestic users paid for their gas by means of penny-in-the-slot gas meters, subsequently shilling-in-the-slot meters.

By 1922 the capital of the Company was £30,000, but in 1923 it amalgamated with the Torquay Company which had been manufacturing gas at its Hollicombe works since 1861. Gas ceased to be manufactured at the Paignton works in 1929.

A new gas holder was erected on the other side of the Torquay Road opposite the gas works in 1929.

In 1935 part of the old Paignton Works was acquired by the Council as a central works and depot.

By 1936 the Gas Company was selling gas appliances from its showrooms and in 1936 an exhibition of gas appliances was held in Dellers Summer Ballroom.

The Hollicombe works were reconstructed shortly before nationalisation in 1947. The works closed in 1968. More information on gas street lighting appears in the chapter dealing with Local Authority Services.

ELECTRICITY

The Paignton Electric Light & Power Co. Ltd. was incorporated in 1908. In August 1908 plans for a generating station were approved for a site at the rear of Dartmouth Road (in what is now Station Lane). The engineers were Purves & Purves of Exeter. The plant consisted of DC generators and steam power from coal burning boilers. The generators would be closed down at midnight and the power switched over to battery power supply. The generators would be switched on again at 6 am. In about 1925-26 when a new supply was installed from Torquay power station, local generation ceased and rotary converters installed to continue DC current.

By about 1935 the total number of wired houses was 6,542 of which 4,690 were wired for AC current.

In 1935 all power came from the National Grid.

In 1945 all supplies were nationalised and Paignton came under the control of the South Western Electricity Board.

Information on electric street lighting appears in the Chapter dealing with Local Authority Services.

TELEPHONE SERVICE

The first telephone exchange was at Palks, the butchers in Winner Street which opened in 1886 with seven subscribers. It was operated by The National Telephone Company. In 1885 the Company were given permission to erect poles and wires in Belle Vue Road.

In 1893 there were 47 subscribers. In 1900 the number was 60 and the exchange was moved to Totnes Road adjoining the Town Hall.

In 1912 the Post Office took over the telephone service from the National Telephone Service.

In 1917 a new exchange was opened in an extension to the Post Office in Palace Avenue.

An automatic system was installed in 1925. The number of subscribers gradually increased and in 1939 a new Telephone Exchange with improved equipment was opened with 1,134 subscribers.

In 1954 the Exchange was extended with a capacity for 4,000 subscribers. By this time much of the overhead wiring had been replaced by underground cabling.

POST OFFICE

The General Post Office which was situated on the corner of Palace Avenue and Coverdale Road, was opened in 1889, but was eventually closed when a new Post Office was built in Torquay Road.

Prior to the building of the new Post Office there had been a stamp office in Winner Street and a small Post Office in Church Street. This is possibly where the office exists today.

Over the years many small branch Post offices have been established around the town usually as part of a newsagents or similar shop.

The early part of the 1900's saw the establishment of post boxes built into boundary walls of property and later street pillar boxes.

CHAPTER FIVE

Local Authority Undertakings

WATER SUPPLY

PAIGNTON RECEIVED ITS FIRST piped water supply in 1872.

There was an ancient aqueduct from Great Parks along what is now Waterleat Road, through Primley House grounds following the contour around the rear of Winner Street to what is now Winner Hill Road to Church Street and on to the Mill Pond (now a storage depot).

A supply was available from the Paignton Well in Well Street and supplies were also available from private wells and streams.

In the early 1900's there was an open stream on part of the north side of Colley End Road, also one at the west side of Kings Ash Road near Tweenaway, and in Shorton Valley opposite Shorton House.

In 1867 a Bill was passed incorporating the Paignton Water Company.

In 1871 a small reservoir and filter bed was constructed at Great Parks and pipes laid to supply the Winner Street and Church Street area followed by an extended piped supply in 1872.

In 1888 the Local Board purchased the Water Undertaking from the Water Company. This comprised the reservoir at Great Parks and water rights at Paignton Well. Following this, improvements were made to the distribution system.

In 1895 a main was extended to Paignton Hospital and in 1896 a second reservoir was opened at Great Parks.

In 1898 there was a water shortage and a decision was made to obtain a supply from Dartmoor at Holne Moor. On July 8th 1900 the Paignton Water Act received Royal Assent and in November the Holne Moor watershed was purchased.

In September 1900 a pump and Crossley gas engine were installed at Paignton Well to augment supplies at times of shortage. Paignton Well was not the traditional well of a deep

hole with a bucket on a rope. Water from an aqueduct cascaded through a hole in a wall into a small pond and then as a stream in Duck Street.

In November 1900 Holne Moor watershed was purchased.

In August 1901 a tender for reservoir, valve tower, outlet filters and caretaker's house submitted by Hawkins and Best of Teignmouth was accepted and work commenced in September 1901.

A contract for a trunk main from Venford to Paignton was sealed in March 1902.

In August 1904 a service reservoir at Beacon Hill, Marldon, was commenced and completed in January 1905 and a 9" trunk main from Holne almost completed. In December 1905 the first water from Holne reached Paignton although it took years before a regular supply was available.

The Holne Chase Water Works were officially opened by F. Layland Barrett M P on the 26th June 1907. The Engineer for the project was Fred. W Vanstone and the Contractors were Messes Hawkins & Best of Teignmouth.

In 1906 a competition was opened for a new and complete water distribution scheme. Mr F W Vanstone's scheme was accepted and in March 1906 eight miles of mains and St Mary's reservoir were commenced.

In July 1920 a decision was taken to duplicate the trunk main from Venford Reservoir to Beacon Hill.

In 1925 in order to improve supply in the Dartmouth Road area a 7" main was laid from Colley End.

Between April 1926 and October 1927 a 15" duplicate main was laid from Venford to Park Hill Cross.

In 1926 the Paignton U.D.C. Act confirmed rights over 8500 acres of the Swincombe Valley and permitted abstraction of 7,000,000 gallons per day. It also authorised the laying of a 24" main from Swincombe to Venford Reservoir and a 15" duplicate main from Venford to Paignton. The contract for the 24" main was signed at the end of 1929.

During 1950 a main was laid to supply Stoke Gabriel and a 12" main laid from Beacon Hill Reservoir to Tweenaway Cross and further extended to Galmpton to improve the supply to Brixham.

In 1952 the ever increasing demand necessitated power to abstract a higher proportion of the flow of the Swincombe River.

SEWERAGE & SEWERAGE DISPOSAL

At the time when the railway arrived sewerage in Paignton was very crude. In a Committee report of the Local Board in 1863 the appalling condition was described in some detail. The lake in Victoria Park was originally marshland where water accumulated. From 1863 for the next ten years the Local Board of Health debated the problem. Better class properties had cess pits or earth closets, but the number of houses without privies or conveniences of any description was said to be astonishing. The Town Lake was used as a sewer. There were crude sewers in Winner Street and other congested areas. Some were uncovered and discharged either into the stream from Paignton Well or direct into the Mill Pond and ultimately found its way into leats that intersected the Marsh.

In 1864 the Local Board sought professional advice and in 1865 repairs were carried out to existing sewers and all sewers diverted to the Marshes. This caused great pollution of the Marshes.

In 1867 the town was divided into three drainage districts, the sewers from which converged at a point near the old fisherman's cottages near the harbour and combined into an outfall sewer constructed under the South Quay of the harbour and on into a 15" cast iron outfall off the East Quay. This continued in use until 1935.

Parallel to what is now Esplanade Road was a leat conveying water from The Marsh to an outfall in the North West corner of the harbour. At this time the leat was culverted by Mr Fletcher preparatory to laying out his seafront estate.

In 1869 a scheme was introduced for disinfecting the water where northern sewage and the two drains from Torbay House and neighbouring houses emptied themselves.

New work on sewers started in 1867 and completed in 1869.

In April 1878 the surveyor was instructed to cover the watercourse in Duck Street (now Princes Street).

In November 1883 complaint was made that sewage from houses in Victoria Square and Commercial Road (Dartmouth Place) emptied into the willow beds (Central Car Park) and was some 18" in depth.

In 1885 a scheme was prepared for draining the area including the Adelphi Road district and to provide a sewer from Lower Polsham Road.

In 1886 The Old Mill and Mill Pond were purchased by The Local Board. The pond was filled in and stables and sheds built providing its first "Town Yard". The Mill was converted into four cottages.

By the summer of 1886 all sewage was discharged through the sea outfall off the harbour East Quay.

From 1895 to 1897 the sewerage system was extended and improved. This included the extension of the "northern Sewer" from the junction of Lower Polsham Road along the site of the intended Redcliffe Road (Marine Drive), Preston Sands Lane (Seaway Road) to junction with Torquay Road by the Old Toll House. Sewers were also laid in Cliff Road, Roundham Road and Torbay Terrace.

The work included low level surface water drainage of Victoria Park from Garfield Road to Queens Road to and including Sands Road, and thence to the harbour culvert.

A drain was laid from the stream in Victoria Park along Garfield Road and across The Green to an outfall on the sands near the Pier.

In 1898 the sewer in Dartmouth Road was extended to Youngs Park.

In 1912 it was decided that the capacity of the low level sewers was inadequate to cope with the flooding in the Dartmouth Road area and in 1913 a duplicate sewer was laid across Queens Park to Queens Road in an attempt to relieve the problem. However, the flooding still continued in Dartmouth Road for many years.

In 1933 Maidenway Road sewer was extended to serve Dunstone Park and in 1934-35 Marldon Road sewer was extended to Pines Road and the first steel sewer was laid to drain Foxhole and Great Parks valleys and Tweenaway.
The main development in the period 1930 to 1935 was the major overhaul of the main sewer system. This divided the district into several areas.
(1)   a low lying area from which the whole storm water and sewage is pumped.
(2)   Four storm water areas from which storm water is diverted through
          screening chambers to the sea and discharge under all states of tides
          under a hydraulic head. The sewage from these areas is pumped.
(3)   A remaining area drained by gravitation to the main tunnel sewer.

A Main Tunnel Gravitation sewer was constructed from Goodrington Village to Sharkham Point, Brixham. The tunnel is 4 1/4 miles long, for the first mile it is 4' 6" diameter and from then on it is 5' 0" diameter.

Work on the tunnel commenced on 30th March 1931. Various contracts were placed during 1932-33 and in October 1934 the town's sewerage system commenced to be diverted and by March 1935 all work had been completed. On the 29th March 1935 the Pumping Station in Clennon Valley was officially opened by Geoffrey Shakespeare M P, Parliamentary Secretary to the Ministry of Health.

1936 saw the re-drainage of Collaton St Mary where the septic tank system was replaced

by a pumping station with automatic electric pump and pumping main to the top of Borough Hill, and the sewer in Totnes Road extended to Tweenaway Cross.

Also in 1936 a 36″ diameter steel sewer was laid from the sewer in Beach Road to the junction of Lower Polsham Road and Esplanade Road in order to overcome flooding in Lower Polsham Road.

In 1937 the Clennon Gorge sewer was extended from what was Primley Brick Works (now Safeways) to the Isolation Hospital.

In 1938-39 new sewers were laid in the St Michaels area to overcome flooding

In 1946 a cloud burst caused flooding of Clennon Valley and the Pumping Station.

In 1950 the first sewer laid by the Local Board in 1865 was replaced.

Also in 1950 the Septic Tank in Knapp Park Road was discontinued and a new sewer laid to connect to the tunnel sewer in Goodrington Road.

In 1951 additional sewers were laid in Collaton St Mary.

In about 1952 two schemes were revived, a new sewer from Winner Street to Esplanade Road and from Dartmouth Road to Esplanade Road. A duplicate sewer was laid in Higher Polsham Road.

WASTE DISPOSAL

In 1863 an offer was accepted by The Local Board from a Mr T Parnell to undertake the waste collection of all houses lying between Fisher Street, Preston Brook and Roundham. He was also to undertake the scavenging of all Parish highways lying within these limits. After the first year it was decided that all scavenging work would be done under the direction of the Surveyor and notice was given that house refuse would be collected on Fridays.

The first refuse tip for the disposal of waste was Gubbys Meadow in 1864.

In January 1865 a bell was procured for the scavenger and in June offal was collected twice a week.

In 1873 scavenging was carried out by contract. About this time it appears that road cleaning became a separate issue as in 1881 tenders were invited for the whole of the roads to be cleaned four times a week. In 1886 cleaning and scavenging required three or four horses and from 12 to 15 men.

From 1896 into the 1900's house refuse was being tipped on the site of Victoria Park and Queens Park to assist the filling of these sites. However, as these sites were becoming

unusable the construction of a refuse destructor was considered. Early in 1909 a site at Sparks Barn Lane (now York Gardens) was approved. Erection of a destructor was commenced in July and completed in October 1909.

The destructor was run by The Paignton Electric Light & Power Company who sold it to the Council in June 1919.

In 1920 the capacity of the Refuse Destructor was found inadequate. Alternative tipping sites became available and due to the increase of houses in the locality the plant was closed down in September 1924. It was restarted in March 1925 but due to complaints from local residents it was closed in October 1925 and subsequently demolished in 1928.

Following the purchase of land forming Goodrington Park in 1921-23 house refuse was tipped there to aid the filling process. Following the closure of tipping at this site tipping was commenced in Clennon Valley first on the east side and later on the other side of Dartmouth Road.

Up until 1926 horses and carts had been used for refuse collection, but during this year two motor collection vehicles were purchased.

In March 1934 a Kerrier road sweeping and collecting machine was purchased.

In July 1935 the Council disposed of its last two horses and all carts and sundry gear was sold.

After the war in January 1946 mechanical road sweeping was resumed and a new mechanical sweeper was delivered in March 1950.

STREET LIGHTING

Before the coming of gas, street lighting was by oil lamps which were few and far between.

Following the introduction of gas supply in 1861 there were 70 street lamps with flat flame or fishtail burners.

In 1863 public street lighting was vested in the Local Board and a committee was appointed to deal with this matter. In 1864 a lamp lighter was appointed. In early years streets were only lit during the winter, but this was amended in 1876. In 1879 there were 110 gas street lamps. A photograph of Winner Street about 1880 shows gas lamps outside Dellers Store and the Oldenburg. First mention of incandescent gas burners is in 1896, but not adopted for a few more years. Fishtail burners were still in use. At the time various traders were permitted to erect lamps with incandescent burners outside their premises. In 1899 some street lamps were still oil lamps.

In January 1905 an agreement was made with the Council and 200 new lanterns with

incandescent burners were provided leaving only a few flat flame burners. In 1908 two oil lamps were installed in Tweenaway Terrace and Mr F W Humber was given permission to place an electric arc lamp outside his premises in Torbay Road. In 1910 there were 350 gas lamps, 80 of which were still with flat flame burners.

In January 1909 the first electric street lighting was provided with arc lamps at the Post Office, two in Palace Avenue, two in Victoria Street, and one in Torbay Road and nine on the Eastern Esplanade.

In February 1915 all gas street lighting was discontinued, following the out-break of World War I.

In July 1919 a start was made to convert some of the gas lamps to electricity.

In 1925 modernisation of street lighting with centrally suspended 200w lamps was provided in Victoria Square and Torbay Road.

In February 1926 lamps at Tweenaway Road Collaton were converted from oil to gas.

In February 1928 200w lamps were attached to Tramway standards in Torquay Road and Hyde Road.

1930 five additional gas lamps were erected at Collaton.

In 1930-35 Street lighting was provided in many new roads under construction. By the end of 1935 there were 704 electric and 267 gas street lights.

In 1937 a detailed survey of street lighting was made and a programme of modernisation prepared, but by 1939 only half of the programme had been completed.

In 1937 sodium discharge lighting was installed in Totnes Road as far as Collaton; Marine Drive and Torbay Road.

In 1938 a 500w tungsten installation was provided from Victoria Square to the town boundary at Hollacombe.

From the days of oil lamps, lamp lighters had to be employed to light and extinguish the lamp and trim wicks and fill with oil.

With the introduction of gas lamps the lamp lighters carried long poles with a small brass encased torch at the top end. Each lamp had a hole in the base through which the torch could be inserted. The pole was also used to operate the gas cocks in the lanterns.

At a later date lamps were provided with clock operated control. These had to be kept wound and adjusted for timers to come on and off.

Later electrically operated timers were fitted to electric lights.

FIRE BRIGADE

The first so-called fire station was in Well Street. It was built in about 1880 over the well with an outside pump for residents. It was provided by The West of England Fire Office.

The first attempt to introduce fire rescue was in 1888 when a fire escape was purchased by the Local Board. It was stationed in the open in Palace Avenue and secured by lock and chain.

In 1889 the Local Board purchased a Merryweather manual engine which they continued to use until 1907.

The first Fire Station was built behind the Public Hall in 1890. In 1907 a Shand Mason steam fire engine was purchased at a cost of £348. It was pulled by two horses normally kept to pull the dust cart. The first man at the fire station would light the fire for the steam boiler.

Alterations were carried out at the fire station to accommodate the new fire engine and a hose tower was built. The official opening took place in January 1908. At that time the horses were obtained from the Gerston Hotel stables.

In 1910 a new fire escape was purchased and in 1911 brass helmets were purchased.

In 1920 a Leyland Fire Engine and Escape Ladder was purchased. At that time the vehicles had solid tyres and these were replaced with pneumatic tyres in 1930.

At the end of 1938 a second fire engine was purchased and this necessitated structural alterations to the fire station.

In August 1941 the National Fire Service was established and the Fire Brigade ceased to be controlled by the Council and in April 1948 the National Fire Service was replaced by the Devon County Fire Service.

In 1973 a new fire station was built in Cecil Road and the Torbay borough Council used the old building for the manufacture and storage of ice cream. It was subsequently converted for use as Council offices.

LAW AND ORDER (THE POLICE)

Any reference to Law and Order in Paignton in its early days always takes you back to The Old Clink in Mill Lane. This description of Law and Order takes up its history from August 5th 1860 when John Williams a farm labourer, had been incarcerated in the Clink by P. C. Watton for stealing cider. He hanged himself by his neck cloth and was the last offender to occupy the Clink. The Clink was restored in 1930.

Justice was administered by the Petty Sessions or Magistrates who were responsible for the

appointment of constables. Special and Petty Sessions were held in the Great Room at the Crown and Anchor Inn in Church Street. In 1865 Paignton had two constables.

The first police station was built in 1873 in Totnes Road adjoining the newly built Town Hall. It was built for the Devon Constabulary and had five cells. In October 1880 two extra policemen were employed.

Petty Sessions were held in the Board Room of the Town Hall from 1876 until March 1899 when it transferred to the newly erected Court Room and Police Station in Palace Avenue. The County Court continued to sit in the Town Hall from 1900 to 1904.

The new Police Station and Court House, with Sergeant's living accommodation attached was built in Palace Avenue in 1899. In 1912 the police force comprised one sergeant and six constables and application was made for a further four constables. The station was demolished in the 1970's and a new station built in Blatchcombe Road.

PUBLIC CONVENIENCES

The first public conveniences to be erected were for "men only". One was attached to the rear of the Town Hall built in 1869 and since demolished.

In 1907 a public convenience existed adjoining the Mill Cottage, but was later removed when conveniences were constructed at the Mill Depot. In 1909 conveniences were erected in Victoria Park and were subsequently incorporated in the new buildings.

In 1909 public conveniences were incorporated in the Main Shelter building. These were improved and extended in 1922.

In 1913 conveniences were incorporated with the shelter erected at Torquay Road, Preston, part of the cost being met by the Tramway Company.

In 1914 timber built conveniences were erected on Paignton Green opposite the Pier. These were later replaced by a more permanent structure. In 1921 a temporary convenience was erected on Preston Green. In 1922 a temporary convenience was erected at Goodrington.

In 1923 temporary conveniences were erected in Roundham Road near the harbour. This was replaced when the old Coastguard Station (Customs House) was converted into conveniences in 1938-39.

In 1924 conveniences were erected in Parkside at the entrance to Victoria Park. By that time conveniences were very much improved with hardwood doors and frames supported on large polished brass bases, polished brass coin operated door locks, tiled floors a room for an attendant and all copper pipes polished. W C partitions were marble and wash basins provided.

In July 1931 a building incorporating a public shelter and conveniences was erected at the south end of Preston Green.

In 1932 a public shelter and convenience were erected at Goodrington South Sands.

In 1951 improvements and an extension were carried out at the Main Shelter conveniences on the Sea Front and coin operated turnstiles installed.

In the same year coin operated turnstiles were installed at five other conveniences.

Also in 1951 a shelter and convenience were erected at Tweenaway Cross.

It is worth noting that what were termed "conveniences" have now become "toilets".

CEMETERIES

Not many people know of the existence of a graveyard in Colley End. Behind what at one time was the Catholic Church and the two adjacent cottages is a small hidden graveyard in which over forty people were buried. Ancestors of the Gowman solicitor family were buried there in 1875.

An old burial ground existed at Goodrington Park which was used in association with the adjoining Naval Hospital. One solitary grave remains.

For many years churchyards were the traditional burial grounds, controlled by the local vicar.

An attempt was made in December 1875 for the local Board to take over burial from the then Vicar, the Rev. F W Poland. An Order in Council had been passed preventing the burying in a churchyard except in cases where persons had vaults or brick graves.

In April 1876 an Order in Council was granted constituting the Local Board as a Burial Board. In late 1879 the Burial Board was looking for a suitable burial ground and in January 1880 a site was purchased at Holloway Hill (the old part of the present cemetery). In November 1880 W G Coldrey, the architect, prepared plans for a Cemetery and Chapel. A public meeting in November 1880 was against the proposal, but the scheme finally obtained approval in February 1881. A tender of £425 was accepted for the erection of the Chapel.

In July 1881 plans for the layout of grave spaces, byelaws and charges were approved. The first burial was that of Mr Alan Browse in the unconsecrated part of the cemetery.

The Cemetery Lodge was erected in 1892 and by 1899 the cemetery was found to be too small and an adjoining field was purchased and in December the revised layout was approved.

In April 1908 loan sanction was obtained for carrying out improvements to the layout,
In September 1918 there was an influenza epidemic in the War Hospital at Oldway
resulting in up to 100 deaths. These were American soldiers and they were buried in an
isolated area at the west end of the cemetery. In 1920 the bodies were exhumed and taken
to America for re-burial.

In 1928 the cemetery was further extended by the purchase of "Cape Villa" and two
adjoining cottages.

In 1943 a further extension of the cemetery was carried out.

In the context of cemeteries it may be noted that the first official mortuary was built in
1884 at the rear of the Town Hall. Previously the Old Clink in Mill Lane had been used
as a mortuary from time to time.

CHAPTER SIX

Roads & Streets

The Road and Street system before the Railway came

THE EARLY MAIN ROADS WERE KNOWN as turnpike roads as these roads had been constructed and maintained by The Torquay and Dartmouth Turnpike Trust. The Trust had been set up in 1824 and terminated in 1874 when turnpike roads became "main roads".

TURNPIKE ROADS

Torquay Road

The road starts from the Torquay-Paignton boundary as an extension of the main road from Torquay which had been constructed in 1841. It was a Turnpike Road with a Toll Gate opposite the junction with Preston Sand Lane (now know as Seaway Road). The road continued past the Old Manor Inn to Fernham where it divided into two roads, one turning west and continuing past Oldway Villa (Oldway Road) and the main Torquay Road continuing past Brookfield House to Fernham, across the junction with Higher and Lower Polsham Road on into the centre of Paignton (Victoria Square). The road from Polsham to Victoria Square was constructed by the Torquay and Dartmouth Turnpike Trust.

Oldway Road

From where it left the Torquay Road the road continued past Oldway Villa, past the junction with Higher Polsham Road (then known as Rams Horn) and past the junction with Shorton Road to continue as what is now known as Southfield Road and on to Colley End. At the end of Colley End the road divided into Marldon Hill and Holloway Hill (now Cemetery Road).

At Colley End the road was joined by Kirkham Street, Well Street and Barns Hill leading to Winner Street.

Dartmouth Road

This road which ran from Victoria Square was a Turnpike Road with a toll gate at Goodrington opposite what became known as Tanners Lane and continued on to Windy Corner at Churston Common.

Totnes Road

From Victoria Square the road ran in a large curve to a crossroads known as Weston Town, where it was joined by Winner Street and Fisher Street. It continued as Primley Road past Primley House and on to Collaton St Mary and Totnes.

Kings Ash Road and The Old Brixham Road

This was an important road running inland from Five Lanes past the old Smokey House Inn to Tweenaway Cross, the section of road being known as Kings Ash Road. From Tweenaway the road continued, to be joined by a branch road from the Totnes Road (Battersway Road) to eventually join the Dartmouth Road at Windy Corner.

SECONDARY ROADS

Preston Sands Lane

This was one of the few roads on the seaward side of the Torquay Road and extended from Seaway Corner to Redcliffe Road (now Marine Drive). It was developed in 1902 to become Seaway Road.

Polsham Road

What is known as Lower Polsham Road was an old road leading from Torquay Road down to the beach and to give access to Torbay House. It contained many lodging houses and the Polsham Arms Inn. The other road (now known as Higher Polsham Road) joined up with Oldway Road.

Sands Road

This road branched off the Dartmouth Road to give access to the harbour area.

Cecil Road

This was an old road leading from Southfield Road and eventually joining the Torquay Road. It contained many old thatched cottages.

Roundham Road

This road was a continuation of Sands Road to serve the harbour area, its extension towards Goodrington was known as Lovers Lane.

Winner Street

This was the main commercial and shopping street. It was joined to Colley End by Barns Hill and extended from Church Street to Weston Cross where it joined the Totnes Road. The street was originally named Wynerde Street or Vineyard Street as vines were grown on

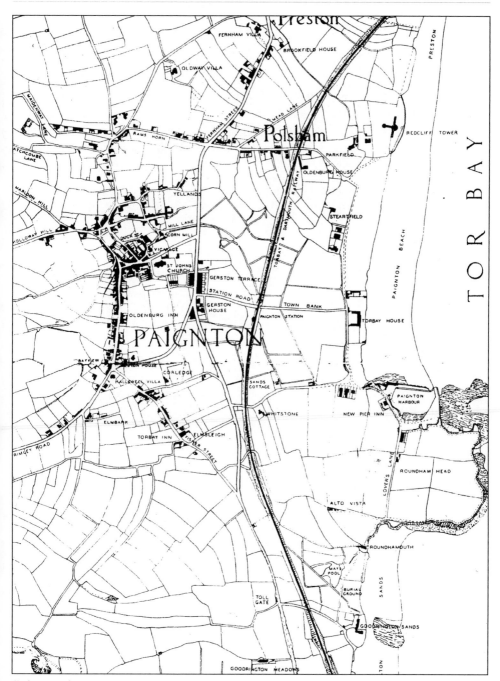

Paignton in 1863

the slopes to the west and wine was produced in premises in the street. Two old inns, The Globe and The Oldenburg were located in Winner Street.

Church Street

This street was known as Fore Street in the early 1800's also as Culverhay Street. It was important in that it was the main access to the town church and one of its buildings was the Crown & Anchor Inn which was an important coaching inn. It also contained the Vicarage which was on the opposite side to the church and was a large house with grounds reaching down to the Torquay Road.

At its junction with Winner Street it divided into two narrow roads divided by a small triangle of buildings.

Well Street

So called because of the existence of the Paignton Well, the main source of water in the area, it extended from the junction of several roads at Colley End to join Church Street.

Duck Street

This was a small street leading off Well Street and later renamed Princes Street. It provided access from Well Street to Mill Lane and Paignton Mill.

Fisher Street

On early maps this was Fischer Street and was an important street leading from Weston Cross to join the Dartmouth Road much as it does today. It contained many old houses and the Torbay Inn.

Kirkham Street

This was a very old street leading from the junction of Southfield Road and Winner Street to the ancient Kirkham House.

NEW ROAD AND STREET DEVELOPMENT

Palace Avenue

The town map dated 1863, four years after the railway came, shows almost the whole area bounded by Totnes Road, Winner Street and the rear of Church Street, as open land. It was not until the mid to late 80's that development took place.

In 1886 Washington Singer, Bartlett and Couldrey formed a partnership to acquire land between Winner Street and the Railway Station. Bridgeman was appointed architect to develop the land and was later joined in the Palace Avenue development by W G Couldrey and W Lambshead. Palace Avenue was to become the heart of Paignton with development taking place very quickly. Early buildings were the block of buildings incorporating Dellers Stores, owned by Mr Lambshead in 1889, and the shops and Lloyds Bank on the opposite side. The row of shops and houses, incorporating the YMCA were designed by Couldrey and built in 1893. Couldreys office was situated over what was to become Church's China Stores on the corner of Coverdale Road.

The General Post Office was erected in 1889. The Wesleyan Church (later Methodist) was built in 1885.

The Public Hall which dominated Palace Avenue was designed by G S Bridgman and built in 1889 and opened in 1890. The Public Hall Company was formed in 1889.

A great Oak was planted in the Palace Avenue Gardens in 1888.

The Police Station was built in 1899, but demolished in the early 1970's in favour of an office development. Adjoining the Police Station were the offices of the Paignton Observer and Messrs Axworthy's Printers and Stationers.

The south side of Palace Avenue was mostly shop premises with offices or living accommodation over, whereas the north side from the Winner Street end to Coverdale Road was occupied by two terraces of residences, some with balconies to take advantage of the southern aspect. This was to alter after the second world war when, one after another, single storey extensions were built to become a row of shop fronts.

Access had to be provided to the rear of the buildings on both sides of the Avenue and this saw the development of New Street which had been adopted by the Council in May 1865, to provide access from Winner Street to Totnes Road and Tower Road.

The road known as Bishops Place came into existence when Isambard Kingdom Brunel built a row of villas to accommodate his doctor, architect, surveyor and chief procurers. The doctor's residence was on the corner opposite the Coverdale Tower. It was for many years the residence and surgery of Dr. Alexander and has remained as a doctors surgery to the present day.

The block of buildings incorporating Dellers Stores extended around the corner into Torquay Road as far as Bishops Place. John Sarson established his chemist shop in 1895 on the corner and this still exists with the original brass name plates on the shop front.

The architectural practice of Bridgman was established over the corner shop with the entrance and stairs off Bishops Place.

The Paignton U. D. Council acquired the Public Hall and part of the Palace Avenue Gardens in 1920.

The granite War Memorial to those who were killed or reported missing in the Great War was erected at the east end of the gardens in 1921. Subsequently a low wall bearing the names of those killed or missing in World War Two was erected.

A photograph of Palace Avenue Gardens, taken in about 1900, shows a large tree, a flag pole and a "monkey puzzle" tree all of which were later removed.

Victoria Street

When the Railway Company built Paignton Station, it constructed two rough roads to connect it with the town centre (Station Road), the seafront and Torbay House (Town Bank).

Station Road was the first to be developed. A start on the development of Victoria Street was made when Mr Foale built his corner butchers shop in 1887 and gave a width of 10ft on Station Road.

It is thought that the south side of the street was the first to be developed as the ground leases ran from 1887 and an inscription above the shop once owned by Emmanuel Beare is dated 1890.

Access to the rear of these premises was by a narrow road and it is thought that the houses in Gerston Road were built soon after as they also backed on to this road.

The buildings were built as shops with side entrances giving access to living accommodation over. Quite a few of the shop owners lived over their premises.

Not a lot is know about the premises on the north side. Trees once lined the north side of the street.

Station Square

The first development of Station Square was the building of the Gerston Hotel in 1870 by Arthur Hyde Dendy. It was soon extended towards the Railway.

The erection of buildings on the west side of the square began as an extension of Victoria Street. The leases on these premises run from 1891 to 1893.

The most prominent building on this side was Bailey's Hotel built in 1894 by Henry John Bailey. It was subsequently divided into a club and a smaller hotel.

Adjoining the Hotel was a corner block of two storey buildings. The ground floor was occupied as offices whilst the upper floor became a ballroom and café.

Another feature of Station Square was what to become known as Waycotts' Corner. The building formed the end of the block of shops in Victoria Street and extended around the

corner into what was to become Hyde Road as far as the rear service road. The building was gutted by fire on July 5th 1952 and was rebuilt some years later.

At the far end of the Square was a three storey building with a ground lease extending back to 1887. It was a three storey building built as offices and living accommodation. It was known as Victoria House and became the premises of Messrs Holman & Sons, Coal and Forage Merchants. It was demolished ultimately as the site for the Regent Cinema.

In the centre of the square was a paved area as a stand for horse drawn cabs. There was also a drinking fountain. It later became the site of the well know horse drawn chip cart of Peter Dimeo.

Victoria Square

Gerston Terrace and Gerston House were built before Palace Avenue or Victoria Street was developed and there was a small open area between the two which gave access to the rear of the buildings.

By about 1880 a few of the houses in Gerston Terrace had been converted into shop premises and the corner had been converted into the Naval Bank later to be replaced by the corner shop of the Maypole Dairy Co. Ltd., and this became known as Maypole Corner. On the opposite corner Mr Foale converted past of his house into a butchers shop and this became known as Foale's Corner.

Lloyds Bank had already been established on the Palace Avenue-Totnes Road corner. In the centre dividing the Dartmouth and Totnes Roads was an area which became known as The Triangle. In 1910 the large red brick building was erected to accommodate the Liberal Club and the Electric Palace Cinema.

The confluence of the main Torquay Dartmouth and Brixham Roads, together with the development of Palace Avenue and Victoria Street produced what became know as Victoria Square. Locals now know Victoria Square as what was officially Victoria Shopping Centre following the development of this area.

A short distance from Foale's Corner in Dartmouth Road was Moore's Hotel which later became Browns and then the Commercial, which was destroyed by fire in about 1930.

Hyde Road and Dendy Road

An early building in Hyde Road was the Royal Bijou Theatre built in 1879 by A H Dendy as an extension of the Gerston Hotel (more details under entertainment). At that time there were no buildings on the opposite side of the road.

This area subsequently became the Paignton terminus of the Torquay-Paignton tramway system.

When Dendy built Paignton Pier in 1878 his foreman in charge of the work was a Mr Richard Harris. In 1891 a block of buildings was built on the corner of Hyde Road and Dendy Road comprising a private house known as "Lyndhurst" and Builders offices, a range of workshops, stables and yard. They were the premises of R Harris & Sons, Builders who were engaged in the development of the area.

As the names of the roads imply, they were developed by Arthur Hyde Dendy.

The earliest development of Hyde Road was a series of rather large semi-detached houses on the west side of the road in about 1893 onwards. This was followed at a later date by the houses on the eastern side.

Dendy Road which linked the new Hyde Road with the service road at the rear of Gerston Terrace was developed at about the same time.

Hyde Road remained unchanged for many years with neat front gardens, front boundary walls and iron gates until after the Second World War when gradually one by one, the houses were converted into shops and offices.

On the east side the first row of private houses had been built and on the west side a large house with spacious garden, apple and pear trees, owned by Dr Ward. The large houses included a house that became Paignton College.

Stentifords (Hyde Road) Corner

With the construction of the lower end of Church Street and Hyde Road this area became busy cross roads. On the corner of Torquay Road and the north side of Hyde Road was a corner shop premises occupied as a confectioners and newsagents shop and owned by Mr Stentiford who carried on business there for many years, hence Stentiford's Corner, but the name expired with the change of ownership and alterations were made to the corner for road improvement in 1934.

On the corner of the north side of Church Street and Torquay Road is a large red brick building which were the premises of Mr A E Day, Grocer and Provision Merchant. It is not known when there premises were built, but the fact that it is built in red brick would indicate about 1900.

On the opposite corner of Church Street is a corner shop which in the early 1920's was run as a fresh fish and poulterers business. A similar business still exists.

On the opposite corner is a large red brick building built in 1927 by the General Assurance Company as offices.

Torbay Road

This road was originally named Town Bank and was a rough road constructed to serve Torbay House on the seafront.

Early development on the side of the railway station was the erection of Broadmead Hotel on the south side (subsequently demolished as the site of the Picture House), and on the opposite side was Nell Pope's Hotel built pre 1871 and still existing today as shops and a restaurant. For many years it was May's Bakery and Café.

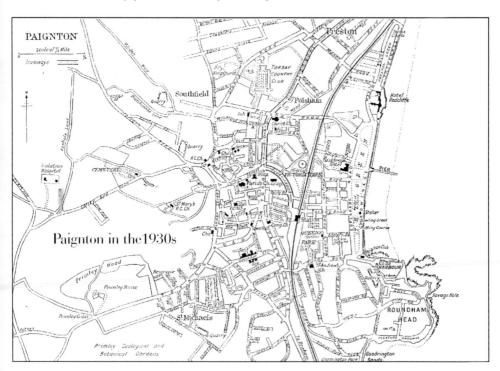

Paignton in the 1930s

A row of terrace houses designed by G S Bridgman was built in about 1869-70 known as Garfield (or Town Bank) Terrace. This terrace was on the north side of the road and extended to as far as what became known as Garfield Road. All these houses subsequently became shops probably about 1900.

The main development of Torbay Road took place in the early 1900's on its southern side. The first development was a prodigious block of shops and apartments known to locals as Dellers Mansions, but officially as Victoria Park Mansions. This was followed by Dellers Café in 1911 and the Paignton Picture House in 1914. Previous to building the café, Dellers had a small café and confectionery on the opposite corner of Victoria Mansions.

Although known as "Dellers" both these developments were carried out by Mr William Lambshead (more details are given elsewhere).

The Architects for Dellers Café and the cinema were Messrs Hyams and Hobgen of Palace Avenue, the architect for Queens Park Mansions was G S Bridgman. All three properties were built by Messrs C & R. E. Drew of Dartmouth Road, Paignton.

Development continued beyond Garfield Road by the building of a row of shops on the north side in about 1900. The most prominent of these was Andrews Stores, Grocery and Provision Store. This store was destroyed by fire in the mid 1980's, but the premises were subsequently rebuilt. One of the earliest businesses established in this block was that of Suttons, printers and stationers. By 1911 there were eleven shops in the block.

On the opposite side of the road was a row of five houses. As with similar properties in Palace Avenue and Hyde Road, they were converted one by one into shop premises. Development on both sides ended about a quarter of a mile from the seafront. An amusement arcade was later built on the land on the north side.

Contingent with the development of Torbay Road was the development of Queens Road and Adelphi Road on the south side and Garfield Road on the north side.

Adelphi Terrace was designed by W. G Couldrey and he resided in one of the houses for a period.

Garfield Road was no doubt developed at about the same time as Victoria Park in the early 1900's, but the terrace of houses was not built until several years later.

In about 1911-12 Marcus Bridgman, a local builder, acquired the land between the road of the lower end of Torbay Road and Garfield Road and developed Berry Square, Beach Road and Kernou Road. The architect for this development was Mr Vanstone who had an office in Victoria Street and was associated with the early water and drainage schemes.

Torquay Road-Preston

A new road to bypass the Old Torquay Road from near Seaway Lane to and including Manor Road was constructed about 1910.

CHAPTER SEVEN

Urban Development and Housing

URBAN DEVELOPMENT AND THE BUILDING of houses are dependent upon three main factors; demand, water supply and main drainage.

In 1851 the population of Paignton was 2,746 this showed a small rise to about 3,000 in 1863. By 1888 this had risen to 4,613, but by 1891 the population was 6,783 an increase of nearly 4,000 since the railway came.

One of the main reasons for the increase was the influx of building trade workers dealing with the town centre developments of the late 1800's.

The number of houses erected between 1897 and 1899 was 159, but between 1901 and 1906 it was 406 and from 1907-14 the number was 631.

This shows the influence of the water and drainage schemes. Water was not freely available in the town until early 1900's and drainage schemes were developed between 1890 and 1900.

The early development had been the building of large houses for wealthy families some of which had their own water supply from wells, and cesspit sanitation.

The first expansion in house building was the erection of terraces of small houses to accommodate the growing labour force. There were two main areas of this type of building; Colley End and St. Michaels.

Colley End saw the building of terraces on both sides of St Marys Hill, Jubilee Terrace and Pleasant Terrace.

St Michaels saw the building of terraces in St. Michaels Road, York Road, Ebenezer Road, Conway Road, Climsland Road, Corsham Road, Manor Terrace and the Gurneys.

In 1906 Washington Singer built Merritts Flats at St. Michaels to relieve unemployment due to the slowing down of the development of the town centre.

As can be expected house building virtually ceased during the 1914-18 war years.

After the war the Government decided upon a policy of "building homes fit for heroes to live in" and encouraged local authorities to embark on "housing schemes".

In 1919 the Paignton U.D. Council purchased land off Marldon Road for what was to become Stanley Gardens (so named after Councillor J. Stanley Huggins). Roads and sewers were constructed and in 1920 sixty nine houses were erected.

In December 1921 government sponsored housing ceased.

In 1923 The Housing (No. 2) Act was passed allowing subsidies to be paid to private enterprise housing. The scheme ended in September 1929 by which time 450 houses were erected under the scheme of which 300 were for occupation by Paignton people.

In 1925 an area of land on the north side of Oldway Road was purchased and new roads and sewers constructed. This was in the Laura Grove, Laura Road area and provided sites for subsidy assisted houses.

Following the demolition of the destructor in 1928 (see page 27) a new road , known as York Gardens, was developed and thirteen houses erected.

In 1930 the Council purchased land at Tweenaways and developed this as a housing estate. The first tender accepted was for 22 houses fronting Brixham Road. Further building took place in September 1931 and in March 1932. Forty one houses were erected in seven months.

During the years of development of Council Housing local builders were erecting houses "on spec". This meant that builders were erecting houses without a purchaser and offering them for sale. This type of development took place in the Preston Area, Roundham and Osney/Clennon areas.

In the early 1920's the land to the west of Winner Street near to the Baptist Church and extending some distance up the hill belonged to Mr Batten who ran his builders business from a shop, offices and builders yard in Winner Street.

Mr Batten started to develop this land by constructing a new road between his yard and the Baptist Church and built two large houses on the north side of this road which at that time was a cul-de-sac known as Clifton Bank.

In the later 1930's the road was extended to join up with Winner Hill Road (which at that time was not fully developed). The road became known as Clifton Road.

Two cul-de-sac spur roads, Clifton Gardens and Clifton Rise were constructed and intensive building of houses and bungalows took place until the outbreak of war in 1939.

Sometime after the war the road was extended to join up with Primley Park Road and Colley End Road. The building firms of J A Procter and A M Procter Ltd., developed and built on 18 acres of land at the top of Clifton Road, Primley Park and Singer Close.

As may be expected house building and estate development virtually ceased during the

war years 1939-45. In December 1945-early 1946 the Council erected six bungalows at Collaton, but considerable delays were experienced due to the shortage of building materials.

In November 1948 the Council constructed the roads and sewers to form what became known as the Foxhole Estate. The first houses on the estate were erected in 1951.

In 1948-49 the first "Cornish Unit" houses were erected in South View Road.

In the late 1940's early 1950's, Eden Vale was developed by the family firm of Mead Brothers.

Apart from developments in Paignton town the development of Preston came much later. The town map of 1863 shows only Preston House, possibly known as Preston Manor, the Manor Inn, Brookfield House, Oldway Villa and a few houses on the main Torquay Road beyond Brookfield.

Following the sale of the Distin Estate, the construction of the new Torquay Road from Seaway Road to Manor Corner, and the link road to the old Torquay Road in about 1930, many new houses were built in the area. Twelve houses were built facing the new Torquay Road and six houses facing Upper Manor Road.

The development of the area in the main was undertaken by the Singer family. One of the first developments was Seaway Road (previously known as Preston Sands Lane) in about 1908 to 1910. A photograph taken about 1910 shows there was no development on either side of the road at that time.

Most of the development of Preston appears to have been between the two world wars. In that period the Singer Estate developed the main Torquay Road and Manor Road and the residential areas of Paris Road, Eugene Road and Morin Road.

Councillor Rabbich purchased an area of land in the early 1900's and developed and built the houses in Kings Road.

The shops and offices on the Torquay Road between Seaway Road and Manor Road were not built until much later.

Development also began to take shape on the other side of the town at Goodrington. The Devon County Show was held on land at Waterside in 1927 and this sparked off the development of the Goodrington/Waterside area.

Very soon development took place and the roads of Oyster Bend, Horseshoe Bend and smaller associated roads were constructed and a large estate of bungalows with green tiled roofs was built

This was followed by the construction of Saltern Road and Waterside Road and subsequently the

Blue Waters estate. The development ceased on the outbreak of war in 1939, but continued after the war with the building of the shops and Waterside Hotel and subsequently the developments of the Hookhills area.

When the Torbay Country Club took over Oldway in 1929, it constructed a golf course extending from Shorton Road up to Windmill Road. The Golf Club House was in David Road. The Club closed in 1956 when the lease expired.

The land previously owned by the Singer Estate and leased to the Country Club was acquired by The Torbay Proprietary Company Ltd., a subsidiary of the Singer Estate under the management of Mr R. Inman.

Extensive development followed the construction of new roads and the improvement of old roads and lanes and intensive house building.

In 1958 the Whitley Estate decided to sell the land in the Clennon, Hookhills and Primley areas. (During his lifetime Mr Herbert Whitley insisted that no new buildings should be visible from Clennon Valley).

The land was mostly purchased by J A Procter & Co. Ltd., but many small builders acquired plots.

This company instructed the architect, Mr C F J Thurley, to survey the area and submit an application for Planning Permission for roads, sewers and individual house types. The main link road from Dartmouth Road to Hayes Road was to be named Penwill Way, after the Paignton U.D.C. engineer and surveyor, Mr Ralph Penwill. Other roads were named Brantwood Drive, Wheatlands Road and Leyburn Road after the names of estates built by Mr Herbert Procter in Bradford and Morecombe.

Penwill Way and the adjoining roads were constructed in 1961-62 and development continued for several years after.

At about the same time the firm of P D Cavanna developed estates at Waterleat and adjacent areas.

In 1958-59 Standard Telephones and Cables built a large factory on the Brixham Road. This started the development of other industrial sites in the area and a consequent expansion of housing developments.

CHAPTER EIGHT

Road Construction and Maintenance

BEFORE THE RAILWAY CAME ROADS WERE little better than cart tracks. The method of road construction was the scattering of rubble (probably soft sandstone quarry waste) and horse drawn roller (probably made of granite). The roads were consolidated by the traffic using it. Limestone had been available from the quarry at Yalberton since it was opened by the Surveyor of Highways in 1835, but it was not used for road stone until 1863. The difficulty was that all stone had to be broken down by hand.

In 1883 the Local Board purchased a stone breaker and steam roller which saw a revolutionary change in road maintenance, but not in road construction.

Dust on the roads was an early problem and remained so for many years. As early as 1863 a water cart was purchased. Another water cart and horse drawn scraper was in use in 1870. In 1870 a charge was levied on premises benefiting from watering, extending from Western House to the north end of Winner Street and from Church Street to the Torquay Road.

In 1873 the Surveyor was instructed to make the road at Oldway passable for vehicles.

In 1879 the Surveyor was instructed to get the stones on Roundham Road broken smaller in order that they may more readily work in, and to do what was necessary to make the road passable.

In May 1899 a mechanically propelled car service by steam omnibus was introduced. In July 1904 the Railway company commenced motor buses to Torquay and in 1907 steam buses commenced to operate between Torquay, Paignton and Totnes.

The use of roads by heavier road transport brought about a revolution in road construction and design, known as "water-bound macadam". The construction consisted of a 3" layer of ashes on which was laid a 9" layer of hand-packed limestone ballast, this was a system where each stone was approximately 9" high and systematically laid by hand one against the other to produce a continuous 9" layer. This was then "blinded" with a layer of cracked limestone broken to a 2" gauge and well rolled mechanically and consolidated. On this was laid a 2"-3" layer of limestone from 3/8" gauge to dust and this was then watered

and mechanically rolled with a steam roller fitted with water jets over its front roller and rear wheels. The road was laid with a camber from the centre to the outer edges where a drainage channel was formed by dressed limestones laid flat 12" wide with 12" x 6" dressed limestone kerbs standing 6" high above the channel and forming the edge of the footpath. The kerbs and channels were laid on and backed up by fine concrete and jointed in cement mortar. The channels were laid to falls to stoneware gullies with cast iron grids and connected to the surface water drainage system. Later the limestone was replaced by precast concrete, but remnants of the old limestone kerbs can still be seen in and about the town.

It is obvious that this form of road construction could not be undertaken without the steam roller and a good supply of cracked stone. It follows that this form of road construction commenced in the early 1900's. In 1912 in order to augment supplies, cracked stone was obtained from Totnes Union Workhouse where the cracking of stone was a duty imposed in payment for the food and shelter given.

In the early 1900's road surfaces were being damaged by mechanical transport and required more spending on maintenance. Mud on roads in the town centre became a problem leading to "crossings" at road junctions such as in Victoria Square.

The increase in motorised traffic produced a dust problem requiring frequent street watering.

In 1909 the dust nuisance was intolerable and in June 1909 part of Victoria Street was repaired with limestone and tar chippings and part of Palace Avenue was "tar painted" and in November 1909 an attempt was made to manufacture tar macadam.

In August 1909 the Council purchased a tar sprayer and the first job was to tar spray Victoria Street. In 1910 several roads were "tar sprayed" including parts of Torquay Road.

Tar was obtained from the Gas Works and River Dart sand was spread over the surface. In hot weather the tar melted and became a nuisance.

In 1910-1912 further experiments were carried out using "tar macadam".

In June 1913 the Council were operating quarries at Yalberton and Goodrington.

In 1916 crushed clinker was used in place of sand in tar spraying, but was not a success.

In 1920 a tar macadam making machine was installed at Goodrington Quarry.

In 1930 Goodrington Quarry was equipped with new "asphalt" making plant.

In 1935 the old steam roller was disposed of.

In 1951 due to the deterioration in the quarried material at Goodrington Quarry the

manufacture of "asphalt" ceased. From then on surfacing material was obtained from outside sources, but in the same year the Council purchased a machine for the mechanical spreading of surfacing material which showed a great improvement on hand labour.

Before the laying of road kerbs there were no proper footpaths at the sides of the roads. The early footpaths were of ash and/or gravel. In the 1920's the laying of concrete paving to footpaths took place over a wide area. Footpaths in the town centre were paved with white clay paving bricks with an incised pattern to give a nonslip surface.

Records show that in 1867 footpaths in Winner Street and Church Street (west of the Church) were paved in Caithness flagstones. Totally inexplicable!!

CHAPTER NINE

Road Improvement and Traffic Control

THE ADVENT OF THE MOTOR CAR AND OTHER mechanically propelled vehicles and their gradually increasing numbers initiated a continuous improvement to the main roads.

Torquay Road

Preston Down Road from Cockington Lane to the Torquay Road was constructed in 1907.

When Paris Singer built the new Oldway Mansion in 1904-07 the Torquay Road ran through the Oldway Estate. He did not like this so he built a new main road and boundary wall. The old road ran from what was Fernham Villa to Polsham Road. In order to build the new road The Rising Sun Inn was demolished and a new inn named The Half Moon was built on the other side of the new road. A milestone in the old road is in part of the drive leading up to the house once occupied by Mr Smith, a Veterinary Surgeon.

The new Torquay Road from Seaway Road to Brookfield was constructed in 1910 following the sales of the Distin Estate.

The first major improvement to Torquay Road was the widening at Hollacombe Hill which involved the alteration of the end house of a row of cottages near the top of the hill. The work was completed in October 1915.

In September 1921 the road from the Half Moon Inn to Polsham Road was widened.

Road improvements took place with the removal of the tram tracks laid in 1911. Removals were carried out firstly in 1924 from Christchurch to Manor road and Tarraway Road to the boundary with Torquay followed by in 1935 from Manor Road to Seaway Road and in 1936 from Seaway Road to Tarraway Road when the carriage way was reconstructed and footpaths provided where none previously existed.

In 1938 the tram track was removed from Littlegate Road to Christchurch, the road widened and a new concrete carriageway laid, also in 1938 two cottages were demolished and the road widened at the junction with Seaway Road. At this time plans were prepared for new Council offices, but were not proceeded with.

Crossways Shopping Centre

This development took place towards the end of the period of Paignton's expansion under review.

It took place in 1963 and involved both Torquay Road and Hyde Road. In Torquay Road Newstead House (once a dentist's surgery) and Croft Terrace and in Hyde Road the Croft Hotel was demolished. The new shopping centre development also included a multi-storey car park and a new post office.

Totnes Road

In 1925 road widening works were carried out through Collaton Village.

In 1931 the widening of Primley Hill commenced, but was delayed owing to a question of land possession. The work was completed in April 1933.

In 1933 the road was widened on the frontage to "Moorlands" near the junction with Conway Road.

In 1943 the road at Beechdown Hill was widened at the request of the military authorities.

In 1950 the road was widened and a verge formed between Battersway Road and Tweenaway Cross.

In 1951 the road was widened from Borough Road to Parkers Arms and in 1952 the footpath to Collaton was completed.

Dartmouth Road

Following the Devon County Show at Waterside in 1927 the frontage to Dartmouth Road was widened.

In 1939 the road was widened from Roundham Road to Clennon Valley and a row of Chestnut trees planted in the verge.

Winner Street

Such widening as took place in Winner Street was largely due to circumstances or property development.

In 1896 when Bailey was developing his West End enterprises a road width of 13 feet was approved for access to Weston Terrace.

In the late 1930's a small cluster of buildings to the west of the Baptist Church, known as Distin's Court had become derelict and were demolished to make way for a row of single

storey shops and an extension to the Baptist Church. This gave an opportunity for the road to be widened.

In 1927 a row of thatched cottages adjoining the Globe Inn were destroyed by fire and advantage was taken to widen the street at this site.

Station Square

Elsewhere in this book demolition of the Gerston Hotel and the building of Woolworths Store is described and this development brought about the redevelopment of the road system in Station Square and in 1936 the old drinking trough was removed.

Colley End

In 1936 road improvements were made to the junction of Barns Hill, Colley End and other roads and the circular horse trough was removed. This trough had been built in 1883 when an old thatched roof barn was demolished and the road junction improved.

Oldway Road

In 1921 an order was obtained for the stopping off of part of Oldway Road. The Singer Estate built a new road in its place to connect with Higher Manor Road. The work was completed in 1922.

In 1950 the old cottages opposite Shorton Road were demolished and Southfield Road, which was an extension of Oldway Road, was widened.

Marldon Road

In 1938 the frontage to Stanley Gardens was widened.

Traffic Control

The first road signs were erected in Paignton in February 1911 when two danger signals were erected.

In May 1913 the Automobile Association provided four "School" signals. Sites were agreed for 24 more signs mainly at "Cross Roads".

In 1919 the Ministry of Transport was set up resulting in the classification of highways. Main roads were either Class I or Class II.

In February 1926 the first white lines were laid on highways.

Early in 1930's Traffic lights were installed at the junction of Torquay Road and Seaway Road.

In May 1930 road traffic signals were standardised.

In May 1932 automatic traffic signals were installed at West End, Hyde Road corner and Victoria Square.

In October 1933 pedestrian crossings formed at Victoria Square.

In August 1934 electronic signals were installed at Victoria Square.

In August 1936 pedestrian crossings formed in Station Square marked with diagonal yellow lines.

In June 1942 the first "cat's eyes" were fixed in roads.

CHAPTER TEN

The Greens, Seafronts and Beaches

ON THE TOWN MAP OF 1863 THERE WAS no seaside development. Buildings shown are Redcliffe Tower, Parkfield, Middle Park, Steartfield and Torbay House. These were connected by a cart track to the recently constructed Town Bank. The area between these tracks and the beaches was all sand dunes. This source of building materials was seized upon by the builders who were undertaking the massive building programme in the late 1880's and 90's. In 1898 the Paignton Improvement Act prohibited the removal of sand from the foreshore.

Broadsands and Elberry Cove are not included as these were outside the Paignton boundary.

Preston Green and Seafront.

In 1877 the Trustees of the Isaac Singer Estate built a limestone retaining wall along Preston seafront to protect the land which he owned inshore. In February 1915 part of the wall for a length of about 100 feet, opposite Manor Road, was washed away, but not replaced.

About the early 1900's Paris Singer completed the construction of what was then Redcliffe Road (now Marine Drive) and commenced building on the west side. He also prepared plans for buildings between the road and the sea wall, but this was rejected.

He subsequently levelled the land and built an aeroplane hangar against the wall of Redcliffe

In 1919 land at the southern end including the aeroplane hangar was purchased by the Council leaving only a small area in private ownership.

In 1923 Preston Green was laid out and two shelters and two grass tennis courts provided. It was agreed that the remainder should remain as a grassed area.

In 1929 the Council acquired the site of the Marine Parade and its layout agreed in 1932.

In 1939 the temporary refreshment buildings and old hangar were demolished and a new permanent café and tea-gardens were constructed.

Paignton Greens, Seafront and Beach (or Sands).

The development of Paignton Greens and Seafront was the result of the generosity of two men.

In 1866 nearly 200 acres of land near the sea owned by a Mr McLean was sold by auction and Polsham Green (later known as Paignton Green North) was presented by Mr McLean to the Local Board on condition that steps be taken to prevent encroachment by the sea.

In 1865 Mr Fletcher, a Birmingham solicitor, purchased 60 acres of land including Torbay House which stood near the sea opposite what was then Town Bank (Torbay Road). The house was demolished in 1877 when Mr Fletcher died.

In August 1878 the Court of Chancery authorised Mr Fletcher's Trustees to transfer Paignton Green South to the Local Board on certain conditions.

It is said that the stone from the demolition of Torbay House was used in the building of Adelphi Terrace.

In 1866 a regulation forbade men and women swimming together, men used Preston Sands and women Paignton Sands.

In 1868 the sea wall and Upper Esplanade was constructed

In 1870 a layout of Polsham Green was prepared by G. S. Bridgman and Mr Couldrey, Mr Dyer and a Mr Crossman. Work ceased at the end of June 1870 with one half levelled and seeded and the roads completed.

In June 1878 Paignton Pier was opened (dealt with in more detail later) and this opened up the development of the Sea front.

In August 1879 a special committee recommended the formation of the Eastern Esplanade and Esplanade Road, also the whole of the green and that land formerly occupied by Torbay House should levelled and formed similar to Polsham Green

In 1886 saw the completion of pleasure gardens and Esplanade walls.

In 1887 a drinking fountain and lamp standard was erected in the centre of the Sea Front to commemorate Queen Victoria's Golden Jubilee. It was paid for by public subscription.

In 1888 a start had been made on the erection of an enclosed shelter with a caretaker room, small public conveniences, and a bandstand on the roof. The site was in the centre of the Sea Front opposite Torbay Road. Objections were received as to the height of the building and this was reduced to 12 feet and a separate bandstand erected on the sea wall opposite.

At about the same time a canvas roofed shelter was erected, adjacent to the bandstand, on the lower esplanade. The structure consisted of seven cast iron standards on the sea side

carrying a rail, and another rail supported on small iron brackets let into the top of the sea wall. A canvas awning was stretched between the two rails.

Also quite near, what became known as "The Monkey Rack" was constructed. This extended over a length of 30-40 yards and comprised of wooden lattice seating on the top of the sea wall and a toe-rail on brackets let into the front of the wall. This was a very popular spot for the lads "watching the girls go by".

In 1892 the first shelters were erected on the sea front, two the following year and the final pair in 1894.

In 1893 the residual portion of the Green was laid out with walls and shrubs and enclosed by railings.

In 1896 Mr Paris Singer presented to the Council a flagstaff surmounted by a Red Indian weather vane (removed from the Wigwam at Oldway) and this was erected near the main shelter.

In 1896 bathing tents were provided by a Mr Langford north of the Pier and in July of that year the Directors of the Paignton Bathing Company met a Council Committee to discuss allowance of mixed bathing.

From 1900 bathing machines were provided on Paignton sands by the Paignton Bathing Company and about the same time donkeys were allowed on the sands.

In April 1903 thirty-two acres of foreshore were purchased from the Duchy of Cornwall.

In 1903-04 the Council made a charge for bathing rights on the sands.

In 1905 the Council decided not to allow bathing huts instead of tents north of the Pier.

In December 1909 the Council purchased 119 tents.

In 1910 twenty-four bathing machines were purchased by the Paignton Bathing Company. At about this time "Donkey Daniels" was running his donkey rides on the sands, a service which he continued for many years.

During the years 1911-12-13 Punch and Judy Shows were operating on the sands.

In 1920 The Council bought 30 bathing machines, offices and equipment from The Paignton Bathing Company and continued the use of the machines until the end of the 1925 season when they were sold off to local residents, many of whom used them as garden summer houses.

In May 1920 The Council undertook an improvement to the sea front near the main shelter on the north side. A thatched roofed octagonal bandstand and small enclosure was erected. On the south side a public bowling green and rose garden was constructed. In 1922

the main shelter convenience was extended and in 1923 the small band enclosure was surfaced and electric strip lighting installed. In 1924 a putting green was opened on the south green.

A few years later a timber building was erected near the conveniences to provide office accommodation for the Entertainments Manager.

In 1926 a canvas awning was erected over the Band Enclosure and this was further extended in 1927 due to the success of military band concerts.

In the same year the Council Act permitted the Council to close the Eastern Promenade to traffic from 1st May to 30th September each year. Free car parking on the Green had been allowed up to 1926. Cars were permitted to park on the Green until 1934 at a charge of one shilling and six pence per day. Thereafter all parking on the Green was banned.

In 1930 strip lighting was provided for the full length of the Eastern Esplanade and Preston Front.

In 1931 flower beds were laid out in the open area opposite Torbay Road with decorative lighting.

In 1932 an Act was passed giving the Council power for regulation of the Sea Front which meant that it had complete control.

In 1934 due to increased popularity, the Band Enclosure was extended and improved to give seating for 900 under cover and 900 in the open.

In 1935 a three span wooden latticed Jubilee Arch was erected on the Sea Front at the bottom of Torbay Road, illuminated by hundreds of electric light bulbs. It was taken down in 1938.

In 1938 the old thatched bandstand was removed and the Summer Pavilion constructed in its place. The awning was renewed.

A photograph taken in early 1940 shows that the bowling green had been removed, a large Rest Garden constructed, and a putting green laid out adjoining.

In 1949 the columns on the Eastern Esplanade were replaced with twin arm concrete standards,

In the same year an Information Bureau was established in the Main Shelter.

In 1950 coloured glass panels were fixed to the lights on the Sea Front.

Early in 1950's a wood and canvas "windmill" was erected on top of the main shelter. It was fronted by a sign illuminated at night that read "Welcome to Paignton".

The windmill was replaced in 1964 by an illuminated feature. The conveniences were reconstructed and more ornamental beds were laid out. The flag pole and "Red Indian" weathervane were removed, but the Golden Jubilee Fountain remained in place.

Torbay Park which is at the rear of the south side of Torbay Road and lies between Queens Road and Esplanade Road, almost formed part of the Sea Front, It was acquired by the Council by Compulsory Order in September 1951 and the ground seeded. Work continued later and was completed in 1953, followed with demolition of central area buildings and gardens and Summer Pavilion and enclosure, to allow building of the Festival Hall.

Goodrington Beach

In 1860 the only building on the Goodrington foreshore was the old military hospital erected in 1800.

At the end of what is now Youngs Park was a house owned by the Misses Brown. This was purchased by the Council in 1912 with over 12 acres of ground. It was demolished when improvements were carried out in 1934.

In 1877 a Byelaw was drafted to control bathing at Goodrington. This proposed "that bathing be prohibited between the hours of 10.00 am and 6.00 pm unless from a machine or in suitable dress, between the wall of the Old Burial Ground to the north of Goodrington House and the land water sluice about 200 yards to the south thereof". However, the Local Government Board refused to confirm the Byelaw. Ultimately in January 1902 Byelaws were passed controlling bathing.

A photograph taken about 1900 shows a sea wall, but no other development. It is thought that the wall was replaced when the promenade was built. A later photograph shows motor launches taking trips from South Sands, but there is no sea wall or promenade.

In 1908 the Council erected a free bathing shed, but this was later removed.

The first purchase of land by the Council was in 1914 followed by further purchases in 1921 and 1923.

In 1931 the foreshore from Goodrington to Broadsands was purchased by the Council.

In 1932 a seaside cabin terrace was constructed at the south end of the South Sands promenade.

In 1937 the "Peter Pan" playground was constructed.

In 1955 a miniature steam train began running on a track on the promenade. In 1964 a diesel engine train ran from the Tea Hut to the south end of the promenade.

Also in the 1960's trampolines were installed as part of the amusement scene.

At the south end of South Sands near the railway bridge was a grassy area below the railway embankment which became known as The Retreat. A limestone wall was later built on the sea side and it became a very popular picnic area with a tea hut and bathing tents.

CHAPTER ELEVEN

Sea Front Buildings of Disinction

Paignton Pier

THE PAIGNTON PIER WAS ERECTED solely by and under the personal superintendence of Mr Arthur Hyde Dendy and his foreman Mr Richard Harris (later R Harris & Sons, Builders),

The erection of the Pier was authorised by the Paignton Pier Act 1874 dated 20th June 1874. The Act records the formation of the Paignton Pier Company, the persons named being John Finney Belfield, Arthur Hyde Dendy, Frederick Palk, George Sowdon Bridgman and Charles Pridham who were named as the first directors of the Company. The Act defined the exact position on the promenade and stated that its length be about seven hundred and fifty feet.

The Capital of the Company was to be fifteen thousand pounds, divided into three thousand shares of five pounds each.

The Act stipulated that the works should be completed within five years (i.e. 1879). It was in fact opened in June 1878.

The Act protected certain rights of the Paignton Harbour Company and the Paignton Local Board. For instance it restricted the landing or embarkation of apples, coals, culm, timber, bricks, stone or slate, except with the written consent of these two authorities. It also laid down restrictions on the levying of tolls by the Paignton Harbour Company.

The Pier Company were authorised to make charges for vessels conveying passengers.

A schedule attached to the Act stipulated the various rates which could be charged for passenger and goods. The list even included nuts, oranges and lemons!!

A full description of the Pier is contained in a publication "Paignton and its Attractions" dated 1885. In 1881 the Pier head was enlarged and the Billiard Room (36 feet by 28 feet) built, connected to the Pavilion. The length of the Pier was 780 feet (including the Pier-head, 140 feet by 54 feet). It had a Pavilion measuring 80 feet by 25 feet connected to a Refreshment Room and a Billiard Room. There was a covered way connecting the buildings which was used as a dressing room for bathers.

Roller skating was allowed on the Pier and bathing was permitted from the Pier-head up to 8.00 pm.

At one time the Pier-head was used by Paignton Amateur Swimming Club and Torbay Sailing Club (later re-named Paignton Sailing Club).

On the death of Mr Dendy in 1886 the Pier was taken over by The Devon Dock and Steamship Company. The paddle steamers, the Duke and Duchess of Devonshire called regularly at the Pier.

The Pavilion and all buildings at the seaward end of the Pier were destroyed by a disastrous fire on Thursday, 18th June 1919 and were never replaced.

An attempt was made in the 1920's to cover the whole length of the Pier with a structure with canvas awning sides and a corrugated iron roof, but with a slightly more permanent structure at the seaward end.

During the Second World War a length of decking and supports were removed as a safeguard against invasion.

Redcliffe Tower (Redcliffe Hotel)

Situated between Preston Green and Paignton Green, Redcliffe Tower was built by John Tozer in 1855 for a Col. Robert Smith, but was not completed until 1865. It was modelled on Indian buildings with a domed entrance lodge and entrance gates. These were removed when the Marine Drive was constructed. A hydropathic plunge bath had been constructed on the seaward side of the building. It was filled by sea water at every high tide and was connected to the house by a subway. The bath was destroyed by a storm in 1866 and not rebuilt.

Col. Smith died in 1873 and it was sold to the Singer Estate in 1877. It was sold by Mr Paris Singer in 1902. It became an hotel and was extensively altered. It has continued as an hotel and has been repeatedly altered and extended.

Paignton Club

Paignton Club (known to locals for many years as "the Gentlemen's Club) was built in 1882. A row of cottages at the south end of Paignton Sea front were demolished to provide a site for the building.

The Esplanade Hotel (later Prince Regent and Inn on the Green)

The Esplanade Hotel, situated on the west side of the Esplanade opposite the Pier, originally comprised two villas built in the late 1870's. In 1883-85 Mr A H Dendy joined the two

villas with a main entrance block. He also developed the land at the rear for sports facilities (recorded elsewhere herein). The hotel was later re-named the Prince Regent and, more recently, The Inn on the Green.

The Hydro Hotel (later The Esplanade) and Adelphi Terrace

Adelphi Terrace was built as a row of private houses on the Sea Front between Adelphi Road and Sands Road in about 1887. It is said that the terrace was mainly constructed with stone from the demolition of Torbay House.

During the First World War the southernmost house was used as a nursing home. In the late 1920's a Mr Purkiss acquired the premises together with three adjoining houses and carried out extensive alterations and extensions and turned it into a large hotel with mock Tudor half-timbering on its main elevation. It was named The Hydro, but the name was altered to The Esplanade when the original Esplanade Hotel was re-named. The hotel was eventually taken over by a touring coach company and the half-timbering removed.

The Park Hotel and adjoining buildings

In the mid to late 1880 a series of large houses were built between Torbay Road and Garfield Road. Many have become hotels by alterations and extensions and have seen many changes of use.

One particular block of buildings at the Garfield Road end comprising six separate houses, was converted into the Park Hotel and has remained as such.

Deller's Summer Café

The building was constructed by the owners of the then Dellers Café. It was very popular for some years for dinners and dances by local organisations, but was temporarily closed for a time as it lost popularity and was altered into bars and flats.

Steartfield and the Palace Hotel

Steartfield is shown as a building situated between the railway and Paignton beach on the map dated 1863. The Steartfield Estate was purchased by A.H. Dendy in about 1878. Steartfield House and adjoining land was later purchased by Washington Singer who built a block of stables and coach houses on the opposite side of the approach road. These were eventually converted into residential buildings. A foundation stone incorporated in the redevelopment was laid by Mrs Washington Singer in 1900.

In about 1925-26 the building was sold, extensive alteration work was carried out and a new wing added containing a ballroom, dining room and bedrooms. It then became the

Steartfield Hotel. In about 1929-30 the whole of the land to the west and north of the approach road was developed and Steartfield Road, Warefield Road, Leighon Road and Norman Road were constructed and many new houses built. At about the same time the row of boarding houses on Esplanade Road between Esplanade Road and Polsham Road were built.

The hotel was sold to the national hotel group Trust House and the name was changed to The Palace Hotel.

Parkfield House

Parkfield House is shown on the map in 1863 and is thought to have been built in the 1850's or possibly earlier. It is contained in large grounds with entrances from Polsham Road and Esplanade Road, being situated on a corner site between these two roads. It originally formed part of the Steartfield Estate which was purchased by A H Dendy who lived at Parkfield between 1878 and 1879.

The house was occupied for many years by two sisters the Miss Coopers who sold off part of the grounds to the Council in 1936 for the construction of a car park and in 1983 to establish a nursery for the Parks Department.
The property was finally bequeathed to the Council.

Middle Park and Redcliffe Lodge

These two buildings occupy adjoining sites on what is now The Marine Drive.

Middle Park is shown on the town map of 1863 with access by a track from the end of Polsham Road. Subsequently access was from the new Marine Drive. An additional storey was erected in the 1930's when alterations were carried out to convert it into an hotel.

Redcliffe Lodge, situated on the corner site was built much later, probably in the late 1890's. It is shown on the Ordnance Survey Map of 1904, but is listed as being in Esplanade Road. It is now listed as an hotel at No 1 Marine Drive.

Villa Marina

This is an attractive residence built for Mr Robert Waycott in the early 1900's on a corner site on Marine Drive on a site purchased from Mr Paris Singer. It is not shown on the 1904 Ordnance Survey Map and at the time Mr Waycott was living at No. 7 Adelphi Road. It was later converted as a convalescent home for the South African war wounded and eventually into an hotel.

CHAPTER TWELVE

Roundham, Roundham Head and Cliffs

THE DISTRICT OF ROUNDHAM deserves special treatment.

The town map of 1863 shows it to be an area largely of agricultural land and it is thought that this was the area in which the renowned "flatpole cabbages" were grown.

No proper roads existed in the area, which may be defined as that contained within what are now Sands Road, the Railway, Goodrington Park and the sea. The harbour is dealt with as a separate development.

Sands Road was previously known as Marsh Lane and extended from Whitstone Road to the slipway adjoining a row of cottages which were demolished in 1882 for the erection of the Paignton Club.

It is thought that Marsh Lane was developed to become Sands Road in about 1890. It is known that Coniston House was built in the early 1890's by Henry John Bailey.

A road known as Harbour Road fronted the Harbour and included the New Pier Inn. This road was widened by the old cliff cottages to join up with Sands Road in 1890.

The road continued as a narrow road up the hill to join up with the access to Alta Vista. This road was known as Lovers Lane and remained as such until it was widened in February 1904.

In the 1860's the Roundham area formed part of the Belfield Estate and comprised the area enclosed by Roundham Road which ran from Whitstone Road to join up with Lovers Lane. Part of the area was sold to Mr Fletcher. Following his death the land in the Belle Vue Road and Cleveland Road area was sold off in plots at public auction in 1878 and was bought by developers and investors. Several plots were bought by the Eastley family. Following the construction of Belle Vue Road and Cleveland Road many large houses were built in the area and occupied by well-to-do families such as retired civil servants, ex Indian Army Officers, half-pay naval officers, colonial bankers and judges, so much so that the area became known as "Tory Island". Eventually the whole enclosing road from Sands Road to Whitstone Road became known as Roundham Road.

St. Andrews Road was built in about 1890 following the building of St. Andrews Church.

Keysfield Road and Young's Park Road were later developments.

During the period that development was taking place to the west of Roundham Road very little development had taken place on the eastern side. A small cul-de-sac existed in the 1880's at the site of the beginning of the future Cliff Road.

G S Bridgman was instructed to prepare a layout of roads for the development of Roundham Head. This was followed by the building of Cliff House and Ocean View.

The building of several semi-detached villas took place in the late 1920's early 1930's.

In the early 1900's a public cliff path was constructed outside the boundary wall of Ocean View. In February 1912 part of the path was washed away and a timber bridge was erected over the gap. The path was finally closed when the Council acquired Ocean View and a new pathway constructed inside the wall and extended as a cliff walk towards Alta Vista Road. In 1976 Paignton Sailing Club erected a small concrete block building for the use of Race Officers. The building was built on part of the old path on the seaward side of the wall.

In September 1949 the Council purchased the whole of Roundham Head comprising a large house with 5.3 acres of land. In February 1951 the house was let as an hotel and the greater part of the land opened to the public. This enabled a new cliff walk to be formed inside the old boundary wall leading from Cliff Road to join up with Alta Vista Road.

In 1938 the Council purchased two properties in Cliff Road including the gardens and foreshore. These were Ravenswood and Wickham Lodge. The latter was demolished and the site developed as a public open space. Ravenswood was later taken over by the Paignton Sea Anglers as their headquarters.

Another cliff path existed in the late nineteenth century running from Goodrington north sands to Roundham Head near Alta Vista Road. This was know as Breakneck Hill to "locals", but was later named Paradise Way. Part of the path was carried away by a cliff fall and a timber bridge was constructed.

Some years later the path was re-constructed and a reinforced concrete bridge replaced the old timber bridge,

In 1929 there was large unemployment in South Wales due to recession in the coal mining industry. To overcome this the government sponsored various schemes to use the unemployed labour. One such scheme was the construction of the promenade and Cliff Walk at the north end of Goodrington Sands. Work on the promenade commenced in 1929 and on completion a series of ascending pathways were constructed on the cliff face. The development was officially opened on 7th October 1931.

The majority of the trees, plants and shrubs planted on the cliff walks were donated by Mr Herbert Whitley of Primley House, owner of Paignton Zoo. The planting of the cliff walk was completed in 1933.

The promenade was officially opened in May 1936 by Mr Robert Horne, Chairman if the GWR.

When completed the new promenade was not connected to Goodrington Sea Front, but this was carried out a few years later.

Not many people know that there is an Ordnance Bench Mark on Roundham Head 104 feet above Ordnance Datum!

CHAPTER THIRTEEN

Paignton Harbour

EARLY HISTORY RECORDS THAT THERE WAS A QUAY of sorts, but it became derelict. The harbour area was separated from the main town area by low lying marshes. A petition was made to parliament to rebuild in 1837. An Act was passed in 1839 and construction was undertaken by the Paignton Harbour Company which continued to run the Harbour until it was wound up in 1936 and the harbour purchased by the Paignton Council. Construction of the harbour must have been swift as the first vessels came alongside the north quay in 1839.

A photograph of about 1860 shows that buildings had been erected on the north quay, and a Customs House built. This is confirmed by the map dated 1863.

The Customs House subsequently became a Coastguard Station and at one time it was manned by a Chief Officer and seven men. It was converted to public conveniences in 1939.

Originally the men were housed in the row of cottages the site of which is now the Paignton Club. New houses were subsequently built for them as a terrace of six houses, Nos. 27 to 39 Roundham Road, facing the harbour.

Many years later a Cliff Rescue and Rocket Apparatus Station was established on the opposite side of the road to the Coastguard Station in the coach house and stables of Kingswood House. This was manned, when required, by local volunteers. The building was eventually converted into living accommodation.

Not shown on the 1863 map, but erected soon after against the cliff on the south quay were two large sandstone buildings. Both had entrances at the top floor from Cliff Road with doors opening on to the quay at ground floor level. This made it possible for goods to be unloaded in Cliff Road and discharged at quay level. The building in the north east corner was known as "the cider store" and its use is obvious. It is thought that the other building was used for the handling for export of the "flatpole" cabbages. In later years the cider store was used as a general purpose store and later demolished. The other building which still exists was for many years owned by Mr E Read. He imported large quantities of green bananas ripening them in ethalyne gas chambers and distributed them to shops all over the area. He earned the nick name of "Banana Read". The building was later used for boat building and as a milk store by the Paignton Co-operative Society. It is now the

premises of "Harbour Sports". The adjoining building ultimately became the premises of the Paignton Amateur Rowing Club.

Near the building, possibly later, stood a stuccoed building which also extended from Cliff Road to quay level. At one time this was Burch's Store and Bakery and later the Toby Jug Café and an Aquarium at quay level.

The advent of the railway began to take its toll on the use of the harbour by commercial trading vessels. Goods imported and exported by sea were now carried by the railway.

However, the development of the town and the building of large houses brought new business to the harbour namely pleasure boating and sailing.

Torbay (Paignton) Sailing Club was established in 1886 by which time the harbour and the quays were beginning to look very different. By the turn of the century on the South and East quays there had grown a settlement of seafaring, fishing and allied occupations; boat builders, block and spar makers, sail makers and later, marine engineers. There was also a forge and blacksmith. This followed by boatmen, yacht hands and longshoremen. A collection of various sized wood framed, clap boarded, multicoloured boat stores and workshops with corrugated iron roofs were erected.

The minutes of the Sailing Club indicate this new development. In 1893 it was decided to lay a triangular course for dinghies. There were 75 members in 1894 among them being army officers, Colonels, Lieut. Colonels, one Major General and two Peers! They probably all resided in the large houses which had been erected in the Roundham area and The Paignton Club was very near!

In the early 1900's shell fishing had become popular with the local fishermen who fabricated their own wicker crab pots, possibly from reeds gathered from the local marshes. In about 1910 the firm of Browse was established as shell fish merchants on the harbour side and their expanded business has continued to the present day.

Early in the 1900's Mr Louis Gale set up a small boat repair service which gradually expanded over the years by the occupation of larger premises. Later the business was carried on by Mr Gale's daughter Stella and her husband Mr John Holmes.

Some years later, possibly in about 1920 motor launches were taking passengers on trips to Goodrington Beach and around the Bay.

In April; 1913 the Sailing Club moved its club house from the Pier to "Mr Foster's Boathouse" on the south side of the harbour where it remained until 1972 when harbour redevelopment took place.

In 1936 the Harbour was purchased by Paignton Council from the Paignton Harbour Company. The Council started to clean up and improve the harbour and Miss Stella Gale

was appointed Harbour Master, the first and only woman harbour master in England. She retired in 1942 as Mrs Holmes.

In 1938 a comprehensive scheme for improvement of the harbour area was prepared. This comprised:-

1. New approaches to the quays from Roundham Road.
2. The clearance of all old wooden buildings from the quays and resurfacing.
3. Extension of the Eastern Esplanade to link up with the north quay of the harbour and the construction of a sea wall.
4. Conversion of the old Customs House (the Coastguard Station) into public conveniences.
5. Creation of a Harbour Masters office from an old building. The work was completed in August 1939.

In 1940 owing to war situation the north quay was closed, a boom was erected across the harbour mouth and the slipways were mined.

In 1946 improved landing facilities were provided at the north quay by constructing recessed steps.

In 1948 the harbour bed was excavated to improve mooring facilities and the area available for moorings was increased. New trot moorings were laid down and the east quay was surfaced with concrete.

In 1948 The Harbour Lights Café building was re-roofed having been in existence for over 100 years.

In 1949 Mr Bruce Read, a local boat builder, designed the Torbay Minnow sailing dinghy. In 1950 the Sailing Club adopted the Minnow for class racing. In all 22 Minnows were built, mostly by the Minnow Yacht Company, under Mr Read, but a few were built by Club members under Mr Read's supervision. As the dinghies were of timber construction their maintenance became a problem and they were superseded by fibre glass dinghies, although one still continued to race for several years in the handicap class.

CHAPTER FOURTEEN

Education

FREE SCHOOLS

A National School existed in Church Street in 1829 with two rooms for boys and girls. It was enlarged in 1846 by the addition of a room for infants and a house for the teacher.

In 1860 a Sunday school was opened in the Independent Chapel in Southfield Road and parents were invited to send their children to learn to read.

Following the passing of the Education Act in 1870 a School Board was elected in 1874 by the ratepayers. It is interesting to note that a member of the board was Mr A H Dendy.

The assembly room in Dartmouth Road was rented as a temporary school for boys and carried on for two and a half years.

In 1875 the Boy's School in Curledge Street was built having been erected on land leased from Mr Belfield for 999 years. It was enlarged in 1905.
The Infants School was built in 1876.

In 1892 The Polsham Road School, formerly the Wesleyan Sunday School was opened. It was replaced by Oldway Primary School in 1937.

In 1895 The Curledge Street Girls School was built.

The last meeting of the School Board was held in September 1903, when education was taken over by the County Education Authority.

The Roman Catholic School in Colley End was built in 1889. This was eventually demolished and flats were built on the site. The new Sacred Heart Roman Catholic Primary School in Cecil Road was built in 1931.

Hayes Road Primary School was opened on the 18th November 1935.

Tweenaway Secondary School (now part of Paignton Community College) was opened in 1938.

PRIVATE SCHOOLS

Paignton College

Paignton College was situated halfway along the west side of Hyde Road. It was designed and built as a school in the early 1890's with a lawn extending from the entrance gate to the headmaster's residence. There was a traditional belfry and a spacious playground at the rear. It was run on grammar school lines by Mr Branford Hartland. It catered for boys up to the age of about 15. It was closed in the 1930's and opened as The Croft Hotel which was subsequently demolished to make way for the "Crossways" development.

Montpelier School

This school was started by the Rev. J M Wheat at a house named Montpelier in Grosvenor Road. The Rev. Wheat was succeeded in 1893 by Mr Bertram Bennett who served as headmaster for thirty three years. He was followed by Mr F L Green who retired in 1956. In 1927 the school moved to Barcombe Hall, a large building with spacious grounds. On Mr Green's retirement his daughter Noelle and his son-in-law Richard Jordain took over as Principals and Mr Martin Knapp was appointed as Headmaster. The school eventually closed in1985 and was demolished to make way for new houses and flats.

Park House School

This was mainly a boarding school. It was started in 1908 by Mr Gilbert at Parkhill House in Southfield Road. In 1910 the school moved to two houses in Adelphi Terrace where it was known as Park House. After World War 1 the school moved to the former Oldenburg House in Lower Polsham Road and retained the name of Park House School. Mr Gilbert retired in 1931. The buildings have since been demolished and the site developed for houses.

Marist Convent

In 1908 the Marist Sisters, a group of catholic nuns, purchased Tower House in Fisher Street, built by Henry John Bailey in 1890. It was a school for girls, very popular, and was enlarged in 1930. It closed in 1982.

Other Small Private Schools

Monplaiser College was located on the corner of Upper Polsham Road and Torquay Road, opposite Christ Church and was a school for young ladies in about 1920.

Osney Girls School was a small school for young ladies situated on the corner of Midvale Road and Torquay Road and it was started in the late 1890's and continued into the 1930's.

Roundham School was a popular school started by Miss Kitchen and Miss Bone. It occupied the site on the corner of Braeside Road and Roundham Road. It was a semi-boarding school with living accommodation at The Firs, a large residence higher up Roundham Road. When the sisters retired the school was run by Miss Nicholson.

The "Kindergarten" catered for boys and girls up to the age of about seven years, but the main school was for girls only. The school closed in the late 1950's and subsequently continued as a children's nursery.

Fenton School

This boys school was started by Mr Fursey who previously had been headmaster at Curledge Street Boys School. The school was situated at No. 4 Southfield Rise. It later became known as Gramercy Hall and eventually moved to Lupton Court, Churston. The school has recently closed.

Tower House School

Tower House School took over the old Marist Convent which closed in 1982.

Brownston Preparatory School

Brownston School was situated at 33a Palace Avenue, midway along the north terrace of houses. The headmistress was Miss Olive Camp who lived on the premises. The school was started in about 1945-46 and closed some years later.

Paignton School of Art and Science

Not strictly a school in the ordinary sense, but more a college for the teaching of arts and crafts. It ran evening classes and covered many of the building trades. It was first located in New Street in about 1895 and managed by a local Technical School Committee.

The New Street premises were sold in February 1907 and the new building in Bishops Place was completed in October 1908. It continues to be popular today.

CHAPTER FIFTEEN

Churches, Chapels and meeting Places

The Parish Church of St John the Baptist.

MUCH HAS BEEN WRITTEN ABOUT the history of the church well before the period now under review. However, a few facts are worth recording.

The Chancel was restored by the Ecclesiastical Commissioners in 1864.

Between 1873 and 1885 the church received a lot of restoration work being re-pewed, galleries removed, several stained glass windows and a new organ installed. The cost was chiefly defrayed by public subscription.

The Vicarage

A photograph taken in 1870 shows the vicarage in Church Street opposite what is now Paignton Hospital. It was a large building with grounds extending down to Torquay Road. A map of 1863 shows the site of the vicarage. It was eventually demolished to make way for the re-development of Lower Church Street probably in the early 1900's. A new vicarage was built in the grounds of the old Bishops Palace with the entrance at the end of Palace Place in 1910.

The Church Hall

The Church Hall in Church Street was built in the early 1800's and was used as a National School. It was enlarged in 1846 and continued to be used for school purposes for many years, and eventually became the Church Hall. It was later incorporated with the adjacent Paignton Hospital. A new Church Hall was built near the Vicarage in the Palace Gardens.

The Church Clock

The church tower clock was provided by public subscription in 1874 and was taken over by the Local Board.

The clock was made and installed by Messrs Gillet and Bland.

In June 1917 the minute hand on the north dial fell off and the clock was out of commission until October 1918 when there was a petition from residents to have the clock repaired.

In 1950 the old mechanism was replaced by electrically operated winding and chiming mechanism installed by the same firm that had installed the original clock. It recommenced to function on 23rd August 1950.

Singer Family Gifts

Sir Mortimer Singer paid for the new Choir Vestries in 1914.

Paris Singer presented the Church organ.

Reredos

The gift of a new Reredos was made by the Chopin Family Association of Maine USA in 1927. Samuel Chopin emigrated from Paignton to America in 1638.

Southfield Methodist Chapel

This is probably the oldest nonconformist place of worship in Paignton and was first dedicated in 1818. In 1820 it was known as the Independent Chapel and in 1851 was known as the Independent Methodist Chapel.

Palace Avenue Methodist Chapel, (Previously Wesleyan)

It is recorded that a Wesleyan Chapel existed in Palace Avenue in 1851, although the entrance was probably in Tower Road. Subsequently in 1890 an extension was built with an entrance porch from Crown and Anchor way. The new building facing Palace Avenue was built in 1884 as a Wesleyan Chapel. On the amalgamation of the two organisations it became the Methodist Chapel.

The Baptist Chapel

This is a very old chapel and is known to have existed on its present site in Winner Street in 1851. It was extended in 1882 and again in the 1920's.

The Plymouth Brethren

The Plymouth Brethren established a meeting place in Paignton by 1851. It is thought that this was in New Street. In 1861 the Brethren had a Chapel in Dartmouth Road on the site now occupied by "The Sportsman" shop. In 1869 the Brethren used the building in Colley End which subsequently became the Roman Catholic Church and in 1888 took over the Gerston Hall in Torquay Road.

United Reformed Church

(originally the Congregational Church)
It is thought that the first church building was built in 1870 in Dartmouth Road. The present church was built in 1876.
The unusual thing about this church is that it is built in roughly squared limestone with

Portland (or Beer) stone dressings, whereas all new buildings of about this period were built of local red sandstone.

St Andrews Church

The first church was a timber and corrugated iron structure built in Dartmouth Road near the Roundham Road railway bridge and first used for worship on October 31st 1875. An Ecclesiastical District had been formed in 1864. The first parsonage was erected in 1875.

In 1889 an acre of land known as Roundham Field was purchased, fronting Sands Road, and a stone boundary wall was built enclosing the site.

The foundation stone for the new church was laid on the 5th October 1892 by the High Sheriff of Devon, Mr Sampson Hanbury. Two bottles were placed in a cavity beneath the stone containing copies of The Times, The Western Morning News, The Parish Magazine dated September 1892, The Paignton Observer, The Paignton Echo and the Devon County Standard.

The dedication of the completed building was on October 5th 1897.

The west end of the Church was completed in 1930 and consecrated by the Bishop of Crediton.

The vicarage in St Andrews Road was built in about 1920. A previous vicarage had been built on the site of the original church on the corner of Dartmouth Road and Roundham Road. It is now a residence named "Ash Lodge".

The Church Hall was built some years after the Church.

Christ Church

Seven new churches were built in Paignton between 1864 and 1961. One of these was Christ Church situated on the corner of Torquay Road and Lower Polsham Road. The church was designed by a London Architect, Mr Edward Gabriel in collaboration with a local architect Mr W G Couldrey. The church was built in 1886 and dedicated by the Bishop of Exeter on 1st June 1888. It is thought that there was a previous timber and corrugated iron structure on the site which later became the Sunday School.

St Michaels and All Angels

Generally known as St Michaels Church the church no longer exists today. In 1886 a mission room constructed of timber and corrugated iron was erected on a site at the St Michaels end of Elmbank Road. This was replaced by a more permanent brick building in the 1930's. Subsequently in 1939 a new specially designed church was built in Derrel Road. It was subsequently closed as a church in 1979 and converted to provide sheltered living accommodation.

St Georges Church, Goodrington

This church was designed by Edward Maufe, architect for Guildford Cathedral and was built in 1938 and consecrated on 25th March 1939.

St Boniface Church, Foxhole

The demand for a church on the Foxhole estate began with a public meeting in 1951. It was decided to erect an asbestos hut and this was opened and dedicated by Bishop Willis on October 24th 1953.

This was followed by further pressure for a permanent church building by a series of public meetings in 1956 and 1958. Eventually land was purchased in Belfield Road.

On Sunday January 8th 1961 the foundation stone was laid by the Chairman of Paignton Urban District Council, Mrs E G Cornford and blessed by the Bishop of Plymouth.

St Pauls Church, Preston

Originally a wooden temporary structure which was demolished when the new church was built. The foundation stone for the church was laid by the Lord Bishop of Exeter on 7th June 1909.

The foundation stone for a new permanent brick faced church was laid on 3rd December 1939 and it received its first vicar on June 16th 1948.

Preston Baptist Church

The first idea for a Preston Baptist Church was conceived in 1922 when the site was purchased. The original main hall was dedicated and opened in 1927.

The building of a new church, designed by the architects Bridgman & Bridgman was commenced in 1940, special permission being granted for work to be continued in the early years of World War II and was opened in 1940.

Church of Saint Mary the Virgin, Collaton

The parish for ecclesiastical purpose was formed in 1864. The new church was consecrated by the Bishop of Jamaica on 24th March 1866.

The Roman Catholic Churches

What was known for many years as the Catholic Church in Colley End was originally built as a Baptist Church in 1838. It was later sold to the Plymouth Brethren and subsequently to the Roman Catholic Church in 1888. It ceased to be a Catholic Church when a new

Church of the Sacred Heart, Roman Catholic Church, was built in Cecil Road in 1931. It was subsequently used by The Jehovah Witnesses.

The Church of St Mary and the Monastery

The Marist Fathers were a little band of the Society of St Mary that had been expelled, first from France and then from Switzerland. In 1880 the group built a church and adjoining buildings on top of St Mary's Hill providing a novitiate and house of ecclesiastical education for catholic missionaries. There were extensive grounds containing nursery garden, a farm and pasture land.

"The Monastery", as it was known, continued its existence to a limited degree during the second war years, but ceased to function in 1971 when the Marist Fathers left Paignton and the land was sold off. It was converted for a time as a community centre.

The Spiritualist Church, Torquay Road, Preston

A plaque on the wall of the church is dated 1912. The President was Mr H. P. Rabbich.

The Salvation Army

The Salvation Army movement was started nationally by William Booth (General Booth) in 1878 and this was followed by rapid expansion during the period 1880-1890.

In about 1881 two sisters from Paignton, the Misses Johnsons, who had attended Salvation Army meetings in Torquay, convened the first informal meetings of the Salvation Army in Paignton.

The first meetings were held over a shop in Winner Street. As numbers grew a small chapel in Dartmouth Road was used for a while and later larger premises overlooking the harbour.

When numbers grew Miss Johnson asked the Salvation Army at Torquay for assistance and a party came over in 1882 to officially adopt the Paignton Salvation Army Corps.

A building was acquired in Princes Street, altered and adapted, and The Citadel was opened in 1887.

Soon after this the Salvation Army Band was formed and by 1913 it had expanded to about 13 bandsmen augmented by ladies with concertinas and tambourines.
The Army marched behind the band on Sundays and evenings from The Citadel down Church Street, Hyde Road and Torbay Road to the sea front where meetings were held on the Green, near the Pier.

There was a certain amount of opposition in the town to the Salvation Army and a local

group of young men formed "The Skeleton Army". Their flag was a black one with a skull and crossbones and the motto "Beef, Beer and Baccy". The "Skeleton Army" fell in behind the Salvation Army on their marches, cat calling at the group ahead and being generally disruptive. The opposition gradually fell away over the years.

Sunday Schools

Nearly all places of worship had a Sunday School erected nearby or adjoining.

CHAPTER SIXTEEN

Entertainment

THEATRES

The Royal Bijou Theatre

The Royal Bijou Theatre was built by Arthur Hyde Dendy in 1870 as an extended part of the Gerston Hotel and fronted Hyde Road. It was lavishly equipped and because of its size was aptly named the Bijou Theatre. By 1873 it had become The Royal Bijou Theatre.

The world premiere performance of The Pirates of Penzance by Gilbert and Sullivan was performed on the 30th December 1879. The performance was attended by Benjamin Disraeli.

The theatre continued to be used for small productions and concerts. It was demolished in 1985 when the site was developed as shop premises.

The Public Hall

The Paignton Public Hall Company was established in 1889 with a capital of £3,500 in 3500 shares of £1 each. The Directors were Washington M.G. Singer, James Alexander MD, Thomas Horatio Hodge, William Wood Ellis, Charles William Vickers and William Lambshead. The Secretary was Mr W Bromham, who was granted the first theatre licence.

The building was designed by the architect G S Bridgman in collaboration with another architect, Mr W G Couldrey, and Mr William Lambshead.

The original plan was to build the Public Hall in the centre of Palace Avenue, but it was finally built at the west end of Palace Avenue.

The building (together with the Badminton Hall) was completed in 1890 and the first entertainment was a variety performance by local artists on the 12th September 1890.

The building was purchased by the Paignton Council from the Public Hall Company in 1920.

In 1926 toilets were provided for the stage and central heating installed.

In 1929 toilets were provided for both the public and badminton halls. A modern proscenium was provided and improvements made to the lighting system.

During the Second World War it became known as The Garrison Theatre.

In 1948 it was renamed The Palace Avenue Theatre, stage improvements carried out and stage lighting installed.

In subsequent years many alterations and improvement have been carried out.

The Adelphi Gardens Theatre

The Adelphi Gardens Theatre in Adelphi Road was opened in 1913. It was of timber and canvas construction catering mainly for concert parties. The first show was Max Cardiff with his "Gladiators".

The building was leased to Charles Hislop for the 1919, 1920 and 1921 seasons with his show "The Brownies".

Records show it was operative in 1935 with George Hay and his Summer Revellers.

The theatre was later demolished and a block of flats built on the site.

Paignton Pier Pavilion

The Pier Pavilion might be considered a theatre; it was a large hall, with a removable stage, situated at the seaward end of the Pier. Paignton Pier is more fully described in Chapter Eleven.

The Festival Theatre

The Festival Theatre does not actually fall within the years under review. It was built in 1967 and Mr C F J Thurley was the architect. It is mentioned in that it followed the demolition of the Summer Pavilion in 1965 and followed what many Paigntonians regard as the destruction of the Sea Front.

Seaside Concert Parties

In the early 1900's entertainment was provided by concert parties performing on the Eastern Esplanade near the Pier or on the Green opposite the Pier.

In 1901 Messrs Wilborn were granted permission to perform for one month.

In 1902 Bert Ellis provided entertainment with the Alpine Pierrot Troupe.

In 1904 there was a concert party performing on the Green.

In 1910-14 Fred Spencer is the name most old Paigntonians will remember. He set up his stage and enclosure on the Green near the road leading up to the Pier. Just before the 1914-18 war he transferred his show to land behind Torbay Road (Torbay Park).

Concert parties continued on the Green until 1920.

Fairs

Roundabouts, swings and coconut shies are what we know as fairs. They have been popular in Paignton almost continuously since 1900 when Hancocks Fair appeared on Paignton North Green. Fairs have continued to be held on the Green (except for war years) for the Annual Regatta and special events, up to the present day.

In 1920 Hancocks suffered a disastrous fire in Plymouth which destroyed all their equipment and from then on the fair was provided by Anderton and Rowland.

The fairs have seen many changes from the days of horse drawn caravans, steam tractors and electric generators to the sophisticated vehicles and amusement of today.

Band Concerts

Early bands performed on the roof of the main shelter, but there were complaints about this and they subsequently performed in the shelter on the opposite side of the road until the new bandstand and enclosure were provided as earlier described in Chapter Ten.

1911 – The first band concerts, when the London Euphonic Band was engaged for six weeks.

1912 – The Blue Hungarian Band was engaged for six weeks and the Town Band gave performances on the roof of the Main Shelter.

1914 – The Paignton Military Band was engaged for ten weeks.

1919 – The first military band concerts after the war was in the summer of 1919 and was by the Grenadier Guards (2 days) and The Oxford & Bucks Light Infantry (8 days).

1920-23 – The Paignton Military Band was engaged for the summer season.

1924 – The 2nd South Staffordshire Regiment Band was engaged for six weeks.

1946-51 – Eight army bands were engaged for the 1946 season and army bands continued to be engaged up to 1951.

1951 – As a gesture commemorating the Festival of Britain eleven army bands, including Guards bands, were engaged for the season from 3rd June to 23rd September.

CINEMAS

The Electric Palace

This was the first "picture house" as they were called, to be opened in Paignton. It formed part of "The Triangle" group of buildings and was opened in 1911. It was affectionally know by Paigntonians as "the bug house". It closed in the 1920's.

The Picture House

The Picture House was built in 1914 by the Paignton builders Messrs C & R E Drew to the design of the architects Hyams and Hobgen. It was built on the site of the former Broadmead Hotel in Torbay Road near the railway station.

When first opened it was called "The Bioscopic Exhibition and Entertainments Centre". It subsequently became known as The Picture House and finally The Torbay Cinema. It once employed a resident pianist and at one time had a 21 piece orchestra. It closed in September 1999 and has since become the ticket office of The Dart Railway Company.

The Palladium

This was an ornate building with an electric organ erected in 1932 on the corner of Torquay Road on the south side of the drive leading to Oldway Mansion. It was promoted by local shareholders who ran short of money during its construction. It was later renamed "The Odeon". It suffered with the general fall in cinema audiences and was finally demolished as a site for an apartment block.

The Regent

This was built on the site of what was known as Victoria House, on the corner of Gerston Road and Station Square. It was owned by Picture Playhouses Limited and opened on August 17th 1932. It suffered the war years and the general falling off of cinema audiences and was demolished in 1986 for a redevelopment project.

CHAPTER SEVENTEEN

Transport

THE RAILWAY

It is useful to reflect on how the railway came to Paignton.

Isambard Kingdom Brunel was the pioneer of the railway coming to South Devon. The first part of the line from Newton Abbot to Torquay was the terminus at Torre where the station opened in December 1848. The extension to Torquay Station near the Sea Front was opened in 1859.

Brunel had experimented with his "atmospheric" railway. It became operational in September 1847, but was abandoned in September 1848. A section of the old "atmospheric" piping used for the line was used for many years on Goodrington beach as a surface water outfall drain.

In 1857 Royal Assent was given to a Bill authorising the formation of The Dartmouth and Torbay Railway Company.

The line was extended from Torquay to Paignton and the opening ceremony took place on 1st August 1859. The occasion was marked by the revival of the ancient custom of distribution of "The Paignton Pudding" about which much has been written by other authors.

The line was extended to Churston in 1861 and on to Kingswear in 1864. A branch line from Churston to Brixham was opened in 1868.

In February 1876 The Great Western Railway Company took over the line from the Railway Company.

The wooden footbridge at the Torbay Road Crossing was erected in 1887, but in 1890 this was replaced by an iron bridge which remained until 1970. At the same time an automatic gate replaced the original manually operated gate.

In 1890 double swing gates were installed at the Sands Road crossing and the road widened. The alterations to the crossings followed complaints about delays to traffic at these crossings.

In May 1892 the line was altered from broad gauge to standard gauge.

In 1903 the station platform was extended and a carriage approach provided for the down platform.

In 1908 the GWR submitted proposals for the duplication of the track which would necessitate the widening of the bridges at Seaway Road and Lower Polsham Road. The bridges were widened in 1909 and evidence of the widening is still to be seen. This double track was laid in 1910.

In about 1911 "Preston Halt" was established on a site behind what is now Marine Parade. It was closed in September 1914.

In March 1928 the GWR made proposals for a station at Goodrington, but not acted upon.

In 1931 the Goods Depot at Goodrington was constructed on land purchased from the Council.

On the 2nd July 1938 the old stone bridge at Roundham Road was demolished and the track widened. The steelwork for the new bridge was placed in position in March 1939.

In 1939 work on the abutments for a bridge to replace the crossing in Tanners Road was commenced as was also piling for a new turntable at Goodrington, but the work was abandoned on the outbreak of war.

After the war extensive sidings were installed at Goodrington together with the turntable to deal with the numerous excursion trains which brought holidaymakers to the town. It was finally completed in 1956.

THE TRAMWAY

In 1910 negotiations were going on between the Torquay Corporation and the Torquay Tramway Company regarding the extension of the Torquay system from Torquay Station to Paignton. Torquay Corporation opposed the overhead trolley system in favour of the surface contact system. When extended to Paignton the whole system was converted to the overhead trolley system.

Early in 1911 talks went on with the Paignton Council regarding the use of granite sets or wood block paving. Wood block was agreed for the length of the track from Christchurch to the terminus in Hyde Road,. The service was opened to the public on the 17th July 1911.

The power was collected from the overhead lines by a trolley at the end of a long travelling arm. At the Hyde Road terminus the arm was swung through 180° and the trolley transferred from one line to the other.

The Paignton Tramway Depot was on the Torquay Road near St Pauls Church and subsequently became a car showroom.

In 1913 a Public Shelter and Conveniences were erected at Preston, part of the cost being contributed by the Tramways Company.

The last tram ran on the 7th January 1934 the service being overtaken by the Devon General bus service. Over the course of the next few years the tracks were removed and the road surface remade. The first section was in 1934 from Christchurch to Manor Road and from Tarraway Road to the boundary with Torquay, followed by in 1935 from Manor Road to Seaway Road, and in 1936 from Seaway Road to Tarraway Road. In 1938 the track was removed from Littlegate Road to Christchurch.

Bath Chairs and Horsedrawn Vehicles.

For some time after the railway came horse drawn vehicles were the only means of transport available, although bath chairs and donkey carts seem to have been in common use.

Long distances were catered for by horse drawn coaches whereas for shorter journeys it was by horse and carriage.

For many years after Station Square was developed there was a paved area as a "rank" for hackney carriages. Later there was a rank on the other side of the railway for carriages to move over to meet down trains. Messrs Battershall & Sons made most of the carriages at their coach works in St Michaels Road. In 1872 there was a horse drawn bus service between Torquay and Paignton.

In early 1900 Mr Hyde Dendy had used horse drawn buses for a service between Paignton and Torquay.

Steam Engined Vehicles

In May 1899 a steam omnibus named "Progress" was operating between Paignton and Torquay.

In 1907 steam buses were licensed to operate between Torquay, Paignton and Totnes.

Motor Buses

In November 1898 The London Motor Company was granted a licence to operate a road car service to Torquay and in May 1899 a Mr Thomas Adams provided a mechanically propelled car service to Torquay.

In the early 1900's the South Devon Garage & Motor Touring Company were running a bus service from Paignton to Brixham.

The GWR commenced a motor bus service to Torquay in July 1904 and inaugurated a

service to Totnes in April 1905. The buses had solid tyres and wooden seats. By 1924 the buses had pneumatic tyres.

Between 1908 and 1910 a Mr George Senior ran a charabanc service.

The GWR continued to run busses through the First World War operated by coal gas contained in a large envelope fitted to the roof of the bus.

In 1923 The Torbay Proprietary Company started a bus service from Paignton to Marldon and Compton.

In 1930 the first long distance buses began to operate from a stopping place in Palace Avenue.

CARS AND CAR PARKING

Garages

Car showrooms and garages (more correctly car repair and maintenance depots) began to appear in the 1920's. These premises usually had a petrol pump. Three of the earliest garages were West End Garage (on the corner of Totnes Road and Fisher Street), Parkside Garage and Showroom situated in Parkside off Torbay Road and Samsons Garage & Coach Builders near Hyde Road Corner. Other garages and car showrooms quickly followed as the number of cars on the road increased.

Car Parks

The parking of cars on Paignton Green and Preston Green free of charge was allowed in the 1920's, but parking on Paignton Green was stopped in 1934.

The first official car park was opened in Victoria Park in 1921 at the south end when parking was permitted on a restricted area. It was extended in 1922 and a small extension was carried out in 1935.

In 1924 the first car parking area was opened in Goodrington Park. A further extension was carried out in 1936 when the hard tennis courts were removed.

In 1952-53 a major extension took place by the inclusion of the whole of the land on the Garfield Road frontage and provision for a motor coach park.

Parking on Preston Green ceased in 1936 when a new car park was opened in Colin Road.

CHAPTER EIGHTEEN

Parks, Pleasure Grounds and Sports Fields

Victoria Park

VICTORIA PARK COVERS A WIDE AREA surrounded by Torquay Road, Courtland Road, Polsham Park, Garfield Road and the rear of Hyde Road.

When the railway came the whole area was under-developed willow plots and marsh land. Part of the area was known as Paignton Marsh and was virtually the town cesspit into which all sewage was discharged. The stream from the old mill to the sea ran through the centre and the railway eventually crossed it in the other direction. This divided the site into four areas which were each developed at separate times and for different uses.

The land was purchased from the Dendy Trustees in 1894. The first area to be developed was the north east corner. Layout was commenced in September 1895 and filling was completed at the end of 1895. The south east part of the park was the last area to be developed.

Three thatched shelters and one lean-to shelter were erected in August 1896. In September 1896 Weymouth Corporation presented the Local Board with two swans for the park, but these were later sold and ducks, seats and shrubs were presented by residents.

By 1900 the layout of the north east area had been substantially completed and by 1901 sufficient area had been reclaimed for Hancock's Fair to be held for a week.

At about the same time an octagonal rustic shelter with a thatched roof was constructed. The stream was culverted with shrubs on each side and rustic bridges.

Later, the area behind Hyde Road was levelled and grassed for use as a children's playground. In 1951 the playground was improved. New equipment was provided with a surfaced play area and a "Brooklands" model car track was laid down.

The area bounded by Garfield Road was levelled and grassed and used as a football pitch. Hard-court tennis courts were constructed at the rear of Torbay Road in 1922. As described elsewhere, the area was gradually given over to car parking and finally the whole area was built on.

The marshy area fronting Torquay Road was partly occupied by Victoria Nurseries and at a lower level was an area used for many years as a refuse tip. In 1935 the area was levelled and grassed and a series of hard-court tennis courts were constructed.

Goodrington Park

Goodrington Park comprises the area of land bounded by the railway, Tanners Road, Youngs Park Road and North Sands.

An area adjoining the old military hospital had been set aside as a burial ground. The remainder of the area was marsh land and reed beds, with a large pond in the middle known as May's Pool. This was said to be "bottomless" until soundings were taken in September 1923.

By the early 1920's, except for three areas at Goodrington South Sands, all land for subsequent development had been acquired by the Council. The last purchase of land was in 1928.

In 1935-36 May's Pool was filled in and Goodrington Park laid out. A large boating lake and ornamental pond were constructed and a car park provided. The promenade was constructed at the same time.

In 1946 the "Scootaboat" fleet at Goodrington Park was replaced with 15 new boats.

In 1949 floodlighting was installed at the boating lakes.

Recreation Grounds

The first public recreation ground was part of Polsham Green in 1873. From 1874 the land was used for archery for several years.

Paignton Green became available in 1874 when Torquay Polo Club was permitted to play on the Green.

In September 1878 Paignton Football Club was allowed to use the Green, but was responsible for any damage.

Also in 1878 the School Board Cricket Club was allowed to play on the Green on three days a week.

In October 1879 the Scarlet Runners Rugby Football Club was permitted to play on the Green.

The Esplanade Hotel Sports Ground

When Mr A H Dendy developed the Esplanade Hotel in 1883-85 he constructed a sports ground on land at the rear of the hotel. He laid down a cycling track of five laps to the mile, enclosing a level grassed area measuring 410 feet x 110 feet. This was used for archery and by the Scarlet Runners Football Club. He also constructed a grandstand for 250 persons with refreshment bar and dressing rooms.

Queens Park

Queens Park occupied the area bounded by the railway, Sands Road, Queens Road and Queens Park Road.

In 1898 the site was compulsorily purchased from a Mr Kellock. At that time it was marshland and osier beds.

In November 1899 Mr Lambshead offered additional land for an extension of the Park, adjoining Queens Park Road and the iron gates at Grosvenor Road were offered as entrance gates to Queens Park.

The iron gates at the Garfield Road entrance to Victoria Park were transferred as gates to the Queens Road entrance.

In 1900 the layout of the area was completed and the design for a grandstand and pavilion was placed for competition.

The building was officially opened in July 1901. It was partially destroyed by fire in 1980 and subsequently re-built.

The Paignton Rovers Football Club was granted use of the Park for the 1902-03 season.

The Archery Club was granted use in 1903.

In October 1903 the Bowling Club asked for the exclusive use of a green in the north-west corner and in 1908 the Club was given exclusive use.

Also about that time the ground was used by the Paignton Cricket Club and Paignton Rugby Football Club acquired the sole rights for football and hockey.

For many years the roof of the central tower of the stand was used by Mr Bellinger as a meteorological station.

The Torbay Archery Club resumed the use of the park in 1919.

In 1934 a new bowling green was laid and a bowling pavilion erected. In 1948 the bowling pavilion was extended.

The athletic pavilion adjoining the main building was erected by co-operation between the Paignton Athletic Club and the Council. Club members provided the labour and the material was supplied by the Council.

Other Small Pleasure Grounds

Apart from the main parks and sports grounds there are many other recreation areas scattered around the town.

One of the earliest was the Whitley Recreation Ground off St Michaels Road. The recreation ground was presented to the town by Mr Herbert Whitley in 1922.

Colley End Road Playing Field was established in 1921. Playground equipment was installed in 1923.

Other developments were:-

Hollicombe Cliffs –	1926
Coombe Valley Park –	1929
The Saddle –	1937
Three Beaches Headland –	1938
Cliff Road Rest Garden	1938
Shorton Woods –	1935-36
Marldon Road Playing Field –	1946

Oldway – 1946. Six tennis courts, 2 bowls rinks, putting course.

CHAPTER NINETENN

Hospitals and Health Care

Paignton Hospital

Previously known as Paignton Cottage Hospital the first building in Church Street was built by the Singer brothers Adam, Mortimer and Washington and opened in February 1891. It was supported by voluntary contributions until taken over by The National Health Service in 1948. The original cost was £2,885.5s.9d. for the land and the buildings. An extension was opened by Sir Mortimer Singer K.B.E. on the 27th July 1928.

Several other extensions and improvements have been carried out over the years.

The Isolation Hospital

The site, situated between Foxhole Road and Kings Ash Road, was purchased by the Council in 1893. The first hospital was a house which subsequently became the Nurses Home and was opened in July 1897.

In November 1913, the facilities of the hospital were thought to be inadequate; an application was made for loan sanction to erect a new ward block and nurses home. This was unsuccessful, but a new ward block was completed in 1917.

In 1936 a new disinfector was installed.

In 1941 a drying room was provided.

In 1947 the hospital was transferred to the National Health Service and became a Recovery Hospital in conjunction with the Paignton General Hospital.

War Hospitals

In September 1914 Oldway Mansion became The American Women's War Hospital catering for American soldiers supported by U.S.A. funds. It was visited by Queen Mary in November 1914.

During World War I several army recovery units were set up in the town. These were; "The Larches", "Coromandel" and "Baymount" in Southfield Road, "Barrington" in Belle

Vue Road and Newstead House in Torquay Road. The invalid soldiers could be recognised in the town by their distinctive blue uniforms.

"La Casita"

The author feels that mention must be made of "La Casita" Maternity Home where both his children were born. It is thought that the nursing home was established in the 1930's situated at the end of Polsham Park abutting the railway. It was owned and run by Mrs Gillet. At that time most childbirths were carried out at home, but the specialised service was provided by Mrs Gillet as Matron and a staff of qualified nurses. Many of Paignton's "famous men and women" were born here. The home closed in 1957 when it became a guest house.

The Ambulance Service

Paignton hospital was opened in 1891 and at that time the sick or victims of accidents were conveyed to the hospital on a stretcher carried by policemen on foot, or on a wheeled litter.

In 1899 Lady Catherine Squire, a member of the Singer family, gave an ambulance to the town. This was followed by an ex First World War canvas covered Ford Model T vehicle with a canvas screen at the rear with holes for the stretcher handles. The vehicle was not available for general use, but only for the removal of infectious cases to the Isolation Hospital at Kings Ash. It was driven and staffed by Council men.

Later, following the establishment of the St. John Brigade in 1926, the Council were prevailed upon to provide an ambulance to be run for Paignton ratepayers. This was a wooden varnished body on a Morris commercial chassis and cost £130. It was described as being a cross between a horse box and a bread van. It had a big brass bell weighing about seven pounds.

Eventually the St. John Brigade had their own Bedford ambulance provided by public subscription, followed years later by the Westcountry Ambulance Trust and the N.H.S.

At one time the ambulance was garaged at the Council Yard in Littlegate Road.

On Friday, February 5th 1926, a public meeting was held at the Town Hall to consider the formation of a branch of the St. John Ambulance Association in Paignton. It was agreed that an Association be formed and various officers were elected. Early meetings were held firstly in the Scout Hut at the rear of the YMCA in Palace Avenue and later in the Reading Room of the YMCA.

The first course in First Aid was started on 24th February and was held at the Boys School

in Curledge Street. This course was attended by 59 ladies and 25 men and 22 ladies and 10 men offered themselves for the qualifying examination. Two men and six ladies failed.

The Brigade was formed on 9th February 1927 when twelve privates were enrolled.

For many years the Brigade did not have any headquarters of its own, but it eventually established its own headquarters in a long wooden hut which was erected at the Sands Road end of Queens Park. The present headquarters, Mountbatten House in Totnes Road was purchased for the Paignton Division, and after much renovation and redecorating by members was officially opened on Saturday, 22nd July 1966.

The first time the Brigade appeared in uniform on duty was at the Devon County Show at Waterside in 1927. Since then they have become a familiar sight at many public events and on the beaches.

CHAPTER TWENTY

Banks

IN THE 1890'S THERE WERE THREE banks in Paignton; a branch of The West of England and South West District Bank at No 3 Gerston Place, The Paignton Penny Savings Bank at No 2 Dartmouth Place and a branch of The Devon and Cornwall Banking Company which had two rooms in the newly erected Town Hall. They vacated the rooms at the end of 1872.

A photograph taken in about 1880 shows The Naval Bank on the corner of Victoria Street which subsequently became Maypole Corner.

Two banks were incorporated in the development of Palace Avenue, both of which were outstanding in design and construction. The National Provincial Bank with the Bank House attached was built on the corner of Coverdale Road and Lloyds Bank, together with Lloyds Bank Chambers was built on the corner of Totnes Road. Both premises exist today, but the National Provincial Bank closed when the company became The National Westminster Bank. It has had several uses since and is now a bookmakers.

It is thought that before the new premises were built Lloyds Bank carried on business at one of the houses on the north side of Totnes Road. Lloyds Bank subsequently opened a branch in new premises built on the corner of Seaway Road. The architects were Messrs Bridgman & Bridgman. A branch of The National Provincial Bank was built at Preston in about 1939, but no longer exists.

The Midland Bank (thought to have been at one time in Palace Avenue where Lloyds TSB is situated) adapted premises once a shop known as "Pughs" facing Victoria Square. It is now known as HSBC.

Martins Bank built new premises in Victoria Street, but the premises were ultimately taken over by Edinburgh Woollen Mills when Martins Bank Limited was taken over by Barclays Bank.

On the opposite corner is a branch of the National Westminster Bank which rebuilt the ground floor of what was the ladies lingerie shop of "Rose and Harvey". A bank had previously existed on this site as shown on the 1904 Ordnance Survey Map.

CHAPTER TWENTY ONE

Buildings of Distinction

THERE ARE MANY BUILDINGS OF DISTINCTION which existed before the railway came such as Coverdale Tower, The Old Clink, Kirkham House etc, but this chapter is concerned with buildings erected at a later date.

Oldway Mansion

Issac Merrit Singer purchased the Fernham Estate in 1871. This comprised two villas, "Oldway House" and "Fernham Park", together with several cottages and the "Rising Sun" inn. (These were later demolished for road diversion and improvement). The Singer family took up residence at Oldway House. Soon after he took up residence Isaac Singer commissioned George Sowdon Bridgman to design a mansion and a riding and exercising pavilion. The mansion was known as "The Wigwam" and the latter as "The Rotunda;" this was the first building to be erected.

The contract for the mansion was signed with a Plymouth builder, J. Mateham in February 1873 and the foundation stone was laid by Mrs Singer in May 1873, The building was completed a year after the death of Isaac Singer on the 23rd July 1875.

The Wigwam remained unaltered until 1904 except that a large octagonal palm house had been erected between the mansion and The Rotunda.

The property had been inherited by Isaac's third son, Paris Singer, who set about rebuilding the property on a grand scale in the style of the Palace of Versailles. He employed a Frenchman, Monsieur Duchesse to lay out the grounds.

After 1918 the house ceased to be used as a residence of the Singer family, a few rooms being equipped as a flat for occasional residence.

During World War 1 the building was used as The American Women's War Hospital and a timber chapel was built in the grounds.

In 1929 part of the building was leased to The Torbay Country Club with alterations on the ground floor to provide a café, toilets, billiard room and bar. The second and third floors were converted into seven residential flats.

In the grounds, two bowling greens with a pavilion were constructed, also fifteen tennis

courts. Two squash courts were constructed in the Rotunda and the main drive from Torquay Road was constructed.

The Mansion and The Rotunda were requisitioned by the R.A.F. in 1939 as an Initial Training Wing and was visited by the King and Queen in 1943.

When Paris Singer died in June 1932 he left instructions in his Will that when The Torbay Country Club relinquished its lease it should be offered to the Local Authority and in 1945 it was purchased by the Paignton Urban District Council for £45,000 and converted for use as municipal offices.

Dellers Café

Dellers Café will be long remembered by native Paigntonians not only as a café, but for its ballroom which was the scene of many great social occasions.

It was a building of beauty and architectural merit, designed by the architects Messrs Hyams & Hobgen on the instruction of Mr William Lambshead who already owned Dellers Supply Stores in Palace Avenue. It was built by the local firm of C. & R.E. Drew in 1910-1911.

It was subsequently extended by a single storey building facing the garden and became known as Dellers Tea Garden.

Much to the regret of Paigntonians the building was demolished in 1965 and replaced by shops and flats. In the author's opinion this marked the end of "development" in favour of "demolition and re-development".

A new café known as Dellers Summer Café designed by Graham Colborne was built adjoining the Esplanade Hotel (Inn on the Green), but has since been extensively altered.

Kingswood, Roundham Road

Not so much a building of distinction, but of notoriety. It was built in about 1890. It was purchased by Paris Singer who sent his wife there whilst entertaining Isadora Duncan at Oldway. Subsequently occupied by Councillor Stanton and following him his grandson Jimmy Gillet. It was demolished in the 1980's and is now a block of flats known as Kingswood Court.

Preston House

Situated almost opposite the Old Manor Inn on the Old Torquay Road, it was occupied by the Butland family from 1910. It was sold to the Paignton Urban District Council after Mr Robert Butland died and was later demolished and the ground landscaped as a park.

Paignton Mill

Paignton Mill is but a memory.

The mill was a rather attractive building built in red sandstone with a large tapering chimney and with two cottages adjoining. It was situated on the corner of Littlegate Road and a road leading from Church Street.

It is said to date back to the time of the Bishop's Palace.

It was fed from a mill pond or pool on the site of what became the Council Depot and the mill tail was the stream which runs through Victoria Park.

The old windmill at Shorton was burned down in about 1830 and the then owner of that mill, John Rossiter took over the Paignton Mill from Squire J.F. Belfield and continued to work the mill until 1883. The increased demand for drinking water forced the Local Board to buy the mill and close it in 1887. It was then converted into four cottages. Henry Rossiter, deposed miller grandson of John Rossiter, built a more modern mill alongside the railway. This mill was subsequently demolished to make way for a car park.

Effords

Effords was a large Victorian (or possibly earlier) villa situated on the corner of Southfield Road and Kirkham Street, adjoining the Cider Works. For many years it was the residence of Rev. James Lyde Hunt. It was demolished in 1958 as part of the Colley End – Cecil Road development.

Other buildings of distinction dealt with in other chapters are The Gerston Hotel, Baileys Hotel, Baileys Emporium, Tower House, Coniston, the Town Hall and the Public Hall, together with the Churches and Chapels.

CHAPTER TWENTY TWO

Clubs and Organisations

IT IS WORTH NOTING THAT WITH THE EXPANSION of the town generally and the provision of parks and pleasure grounds, many social and sports clubs and other organisations came into being.

SOCIAL CLUBS

The PAIGNTON CLUB, described in more detail elsewhere, was built in 1882 to cater for "the gentry" who had built large villas in the Roundham Road, Belle Vue area. It contained all the facilities of a social club such as bar, billiard room, card room, etc. It has continued to flourish to the present day.

The Constitutional Club

This building was incorporated in the development of the south side of Palace Avenue in the late 1800's and bears the name inscribed over the entrance. It later became the Conservative Club and incorporated all the requirements of a social club.

THE LIBERAL CLUB was built in 1910 in Victoria Square between the Totnes and Dartmouth Roads, but ceased to be a club many years later.

THE TORBAY CLUB was established in the early 1920's in part of the old Bijou Theatre complex in Hyde Road. The entrance was off the small road leading to Victoria Park. It contained bars, billiard room, card room etc and was very popular with builders, business and professional men who found it very convenient for a lunch time break. It ceased to exist when the whole block was demolished and rebuilt.

The TORBAY COUNTRY CLUB was established at Oldway Mansion in the early 1930's and functioned as a social club and sports club. Some years later it laid out a golf course on the sloping ground between Shorton Road and Windmill Lane with an approach road opposite Westhill Road and a Golf Club House. The property was on lease from the Oldway Estate and when Paris Singer died in 1932 he willed that when the Country Club lease expired the property should be offered to the Local Authority. The Club did not operate during World War II as the buildings were taken over by the R.A.F.

Preston Conservative Club

This was erected on land on Torquay Road donated by Mr Robert Butland of Preston House and was opened in 1929.

SPORTS CLUBS

These are too numerous to describe in detail, only a brief description of each being given. Each came into being as facilities became available.

The earliest facility was the establishment of the Cycling Track and sports ground at the rear of the Esplanade Hotel (now Inn on the Green) in 1883. This saw the formation of the football club known as The Scarlet Runners.

The building of Paignton Pier in 1878 provided facilities for headquarters for swimming and sailing. The Paignton Amateur Swimming and Life Saving Club and The Torbay Sailing Club (later Paignton Sailing Club) established headquarters at the seaward end of the Pier. The Swimming Club subsequently had a wooden changing room on the beach near the Pier.

It is recorded that the Torbay Sailing Club was established in 1886. Its burgee "red and white chequered with anchor in centre" was adopted in 1894. In April 1913 the Club moved from the Pier to Mr Foster's Boathouse on the south side of Paignton Harbour. The Club purchased the premises in 1934 and converted it into a Clubhouse. In 1968 following the formation of the County Borough of Torbay, it was decided to alter the title to Paignton Sailing Club to identify it as being a Paignton Club. In 1972 the Local Authority decided to go ahead with a Harbour Development Scheme which involved the demolition of all the old timber buildings on the south side and erection of new buildings. The Sailing Club took over part of the development and its new premises were opened by Mr Denis Howell M.P., Minister for Sport and Recreation in August 1975. There were 75 members in 1894 and over 300 by 1975.

Two other clubs became established on the harbour side; The Sea Angling Club and the Paignton Amateur Rowing Club. The Rowing Club still occupies the building which has been their headquarters from the beginning. They purchased the boat house in 1930 for £500. The Sea Anglers started off in a timber building, then moved into part of the new buildings, but eventually moved into what was a large residence, named Ravenswood, in Cliff Road.

Paignton Rugby Football Club

The author has been privileged by the Paignton Rugby Club to see a copy of an article written by C. H. Patterson in 1973 entitled "A Century of Rugby at Paignton, 1873-1973.

In it he traces the start of organised rugby in Paignton in 1873. Rugby had been played in Paignton as early as 1870 when there was a team know as "The Blues". This continued until about 1887 when "The Scarlet Runners" came into existence as a recognised club.

Matches were first played on the sports ground built by A.H. Dendy at the rear of what was then known as the Esplanade Hotel, and occasionally in a field at Preston. Later all games were played on The Green until the construction of Queens Park (see Chapter 18).

The first game in Queens Park took place on October 4th 1902.

For some time the club had been known as Paignton Football Club, but on March 3rd 1914 a meeting took place at the Gerston Hotel to consider the formation of a Paignton Rugby Club. However on the outbreak of war in 1914 the game was brought to a standstill. The Club was revived in January 1919 and has continued to prosper over the ensuing years.

Paignton (Torbay) Rifle and Pistol Club

In 1901 Mr W. G. Singer gave land at Blagdon to be used as a range by the Paignton Volunteers Company, 1st Division Voluntary Artillery. The range was fitted out by H. Matthews and Sons, The Gun Shop, 101-105 Winner Street.

This was followed by an invitation in the Paignton Observer inviting persons interested in joining a Paignton Rifle Club which was in the process of being formed.

At the end of 1901 a meeting of the Paignton Rifle Club was held at the Drill Hall attached to the Public Hall in Palace Avenue.

The Club has continued to flourish over the years and has used a number of ranges and in about 1960 built a Club House and Indoor Range on a site on the corner of Dartmouth Road and what is now Penwill Way.

Other Sports Clubs

The following is a list of sports clubs which came into existence when facilities became available.

Paignton Green:	Football (various clubs)
Victoria Park:	Football (various clubs)
Queens Park:	Paignton Archery Club
	Paignton Bowling Club (established in 1902)
	Paignton Rugby Football Club
	(moved into Queens Park in 1902)
	Paignton Cricket Club
	(also moved into Queens Park in about 1902)
	Paignton Amateur Athletic Club

Paignton Hockey Club

Tennis Clubs

The Badminton Club used the Badminton Hall, part of The Public Hall.

YOUTH ORGANISATIONS

The Y.M.C.A.

The Y.M.C.A. formed part of the row of buildings built on the south side of Palace Avenue in 1893. The Association subsequently built new premises on Dartmouth Road overlooking Clennon Valley.

The Boy Scouts

The Boy Scout movement was started by Robert Baden Powell. He was born in 1857 and served in the British Army in India, Afghanistan and South Africa. In 1908 he published a book entitled "Scouting for Boys" and at about that time founded the Boy Scouts. Information on the establishment and growth of the Scout movement in Paignton is very scanty.

Over a period of many years a number of scout troops have existed as below, the majority being associated with churches.

1st Paignton Troop	-	YMCA
2nd Paignton Troop	-	Roman Catholic Church
3rd Paignton Troop	-	Collaton St Mary
4th Paignton Troop	-	Park House School
5th Paignton Troop	-	(Coverdale) Paignton Parish Church
6th Paignton Troop	-	See later under Sea Scouts
7th Paignton Troop	-	Christ Church
8th Paignton Troop	-	Montpelier School
9th Paignton Troop	-	St Michaels Church
10th Paignton Troop	-	St Pauls Church
11th Paignton Troop	-	Methodist Church Palace Avenue

It is thought the 1st Paignton Troop was established soon after World War I. For many years the headquarters was a large timber hut at the rear of the then Y.M.C.A. premises in Palace Avenue. The 6th Troop (later Sea Scouts) was established in 1922 so it follows that the lower numbered troops were established before that date.

Membership of the 8th troop at Montpelier School was a compulsory Saturday activity and at one time numbered over 150 cubs and scouts. It is thought that the troop was established in about 1927 when the school moved into Barcombe Hall.

The number of troops has declined over the years and, in addition to the Sea Scouts, only the 10th and 11th troops exist.

Sea Scouts

What is now named the 6th Torbay "Britannia" Sea Scout Group started in December 1922 as The 6th Paignton Scout Troop.

The troop met in the Congregational Church Hall in Dartmouth Road and the Church Minister, the Rev. W. M. Worsam, was the first scout master.

In 1924 a scout cub pack for boys aged 8 to 11 was formed with Mrs L. Davies Grylls as their leader.

In about 1929 the Rev. Worsam left the district and Mr Ashplant, a local blacksmith, took over as scout master.

In 1932 the headquarters moved to the British Legion Hall in Grosvenor Road and church parades were held at St Michaels Church. Rover scout E. Parnell became Scout Master.

In 1933 Mrs Davies Grylls left the town and Mr A. Wallis took over as cub leader.

In 1934 the group were presented with their first set of colours and these were dedicated at St. Michaels Church.

From 1935 to 1941 there were several scout leaders who worked at the Dartmouth Royal Naval College and boating activities were started in 1935.

On St Georges Day 1936 the group changed its name to the 6th Paignton Sea Scouts. The group moved its headquarters to the Drill Hall in York Road.

In 1937, Mr G.H.K. Kingdon, a keen yachtsman and past chairman of Paignton U.D.C., purchased a leasehold hut at Paignton Harbour as the scout headquarters and also provided an ex-naval 32ft. sailing cutter christened "Spray". The hut was next to Mr Louis Gale's boatyard and was very basic with no heat, light or water.

On the outbreak of war in 1939 the harbour was fenced off and all boating ceased.

By 1941 all the leaders had been "called up" and patrol leaders ran the activities.

During 1942 the group became "Admiralty Recognised" as a pre war service unit subject to inspection every year by an Admiralty representative. The first inspection was made by Commander W.L. Rossiter, R.N.R. on 20th April 1942.

In 1948 the sea scouts manned tenders for yachtsmen at the Sailing Olympics in Torbay and this led to increased interest in sailing and other marine activities.

In 1949 the group acquired an ex-naval whaler "Endeavour" and she remained in use until in 1955 when she came to a sad end off Torquay in a S.W. gale.

In 1963 two new boats were launched.

In 1967 the name of the group was changed to the 6th Torbay on account of the formation of the Torbay County Borough.

In 1971 the name Britannia was given to the group by the Royal Naval College, Dartmouth.

In 1973 the old timber premises were demolished and new permanent headquarters erected.

Today the group has a total of over 150 members of various ages.

The Girl Guides

The Girl Guide movement in Paignton was started by the setting up of a Local Association Executive Committee. Following a meeting of the Executive Committee on December 8th 1917 it was agreed on December 7th 1918 to register the 1st Paignton Senior Patrol, the 2nd Paignton Guides and the 1st Paignton Brownies. A certificate of Registration was received in January 1919.

Three rooms were rented as headquarters on the top floor of 44 Victoria Street from the Plymouth Brewery Company. The lease was for twelve months from 1st February 1919. By July 1920 the rooms had been vacated and three rooms rented at the Y.M.C.A. in Palace Avenue.

By April 1921 the Y.M.C.A. had been vacated and the Executive Committee held its meetings at Sunneycroft House in Hyde Road and later at Whitstone House in Whitstone Road where it remained for many years.

The Guide Companies were attached to local churches and chapels and held their meetings in church halls.

In January 1922 Mr Frank Rossiter offered the Committee a plot of land behind Polsham Park with access from Lower Polsham Road at a rent of £6 per year on a 7, 14 or 21 year lease. The offer was accepted and a hut was purchased for £122. There was no drainage or other services available and these had to be installed.

By October 1924 the hut had been erected and it was decided it would be a District Hut available to all companies.

"The Hut" was officially opened by Lady Clinton on March 20th 1925.

From the beginning "The Hut" was a constant financial embarrassment in maintenance, heating, lighting and equipment, but was constantly in use for social occasions and meetings. It was eventually sold at the end of 1942 for a nett sum of £63 10s 6d.

In May 1924 it was reported that a Ranger Company had been formed, In 1941 the 1st Paignton Rangers was formed, its headquarters being "The Hut". It comprised a Land Section and a Sea Section.

The Rangers were very active during the war years in dealing with evacuees, pea picking and potato digging, cultivating a vegetable patch, arranging social evenings for service men billeted in the area, arranging "goodies" parcels for sending to local service men and prisoners of war, undertaking Civil Defence duties and knitting mitts, socks and balaclavas.

Many of the Rangers joined the armed forces and this reduced the numbers and the "Land Rangers" was disbanded in July 1943. The Sea Rangers continued to exist as described later.

The Brownies formed an important section in the Girl Guide Movement. The 1st Paignton Brownies was registered in 1919 and were reported as flourishing using Church halls. When Lady Baden Powell visited Paignton in March 1943 the Brownies formed an arch to welcome her.

The development of the Guide movement in Paignton can be noted by the figures quoted at Executive Committee Meetings on various occasions. In May 1924 the total was 154, in April 1946 the total was 277 and in 1955 there were 331 members. The numbers continued to be over 300 until well into the 1960's.

Sea Rangers

As early as 1924 the Sea Rangers formed part of the local Girl Guides Association. In November 1931 the Sea Ranger Patrol was attached to the VIII Girl Guide Company.

In 1941 a separate Sea Ranger Company was formed by Miss K Baker. Miss Baker remained in charge of the Sea Rangers for many years and for a long period was the Girl Guide District Commissioner.

On the 10th March 1942 the Sea Rangers launched the Sea Ranger Ship "Daring Pilot".

In 1943 when Lady Bowden Powell visited Paignton the Sea Rangers "piped" her in.

In 1946 Miss Baker reported that the Sea Rangers had purchased a "whaler" for £27. By this date restrictions on the use of the harbour had been lifted and the Sea Rangers set up their headquarters in a hut on the south side of the harbour.

The Sea Rangers continued to flourish as part of the Girl Guide movement and in 1959 it

was reported that it had 27 members. In 1963 they celebrated their 21st birthday and in May 1967 celebrated their 25th birthday by launching a "gig" named Cycleen.

Miss Baker resigned in 1969.

Boys Brigade

The 1st Paignton Boys Brigade was formed in 1926 under Mr A Mathews at Southfield Methodist Church. It started with 16 boys and 4 officers, but within two years grew to 40 boys and 6 officers. They then transferred to the Queens Park Pavilion by which time they had formed a band.

OTHER ORGANISATIONS

Paignton Rotary Club

The Paignton Rotary Club was founded in 1926 and held its weekly meetings at Dellers Café upper ballroom until the café was demolished in 1963 when it moved its meeting room to The Harbour Lights Restaurant.

Freemasons

The Torbay Lodge of Freemasons No. 1358 was granted its warrant in May 1871 to meet at the newly built Town Hall. The Lodge was consecrated in August 1871 and occupied three rooms upstairs in the Town Hall. The first meeting was held in August 1872. In 1890 G. S. Bridgman gave a site for premises in what is now Courtland Road and the new Lodge Temple, designed by G.S. Bridgman and erected by Mr Rabbich was consecrated in August 1891. It was registered as a Club in 1903. Various daughter lodges and degrees were subsequently consecrated, the last being Quest Lodge in 1963.

Oddfellows

It is not known when the Oddfellows were established in Paignton. It is known that the Good Samaritan Lodge was revitalised after the Second World War by Gilbert Mudge who was made Permanent Secretary in 1949, a position he held until 1994.

The St Andrews Boys Bible Class &
The St Margaret's Old Boys Association

The St Andrews Boys Bible Class was started by Miss Ethel Kate Bradford in about 1908 catering for boys between the ages of 14 and 18. meeting on Sunday afternoons in the Church Hall. She also started a club for the benefit of the boys which was called St

Margaret's (after the name of her house in Manor Road). At one time there were as many as 50 boys in the class. A football team was formed which played in the local league. Her first and foremost rule of membership was regular attendances at Holy Communion on the first Sunday of the month. She died in 1972 at the age of 90.

In February 1960 former members of the St Margaret's Club decided to form the St Margaret's Old Boys Association and the first re-union was held in April 1961. Since then, there has been a re-union luncheon meeting every year. In December 1961 the first edition of a magazine entitled "The St Margaret's Review", contained contributions from members, was circulated to all members and has continued to be circulated for many years.

CHAPTER TWENTY THREE

The Retail Trades

PRE 1860 ALL SHOPS AND BUSINESSES were concentrated along the main streets then in existence, namely Church Street, Culverhay Street and Winner Street.

The businesses centred around the everyday needs of the population such as butchers, bakers, tailors, dress makers, bonnet makers, straw hat makers, blacksmiths, saddlers, chemists, boot makers and one watchmaker. There were five inns in the area.

The character of these streets has not altered much today, except for the disappearance of the smaller shops such as tailors, dressmakers, bonnet makers and the like.

Mr Bailey built his Emporium at Weston (West End) at the end of Winner Street, but it was never very successful, being a little too far out of the town. It is now a Billiard and Snooker Hall.

At the turn of the century two Italian families settled in Winner Street; the Pelosi family and the Dimeo family. The Pelosi family began the production of ice cream on a commercial basis, a common sight was a horse drawn ice cream cart manned by either of the two brothers Peter and George. Subsequently the family opened ice cream parlours in Torbay Road and elsewhere.

The Dimeo family started a fried chip business adjacent to the Pelosis. Later after the Picture House was opened a familiar sight was a horse drawn chip cart in Station Square with flames roaring from its metal chimney. "Only best hotel dripping used" was the slogan painted on the side of the cart.

Two businesses which have flourished from a small beginning are the Co-op and Dellers.

The Paignton Co-operative Society was established in Winner Street in the early 1900's, but in 1906 many old buildings were demolished and a large building erected on the site. Iron letters on the front of the building spell out P C S 1906. The new building comprised a large grocery and provision department on the ground floor with ladies and children's dress shop adjoining.

On the first floor were offices, which included the Savings Bank, and on the second floor was the Co-operative Hall which was used for meetings and social gatherings.

The Society still retained premises on the north side as a dairy and on the south side a Boot and Shoe shop and a Haberdashers Shop.

The activities of the Society expanded greatly in the first half of 1900. It acquired Great Parks Farm which supplied a flourishing dairy business adjoining the main store. It supplied milk and dairy produce to Colley End and other districts by a pony drawn milk float fitted with a large churn and measuring jugs.

The Society opened a Poultry and Fishmongers Department on the opposite side of the street and later a Butcher's Shop on the corner of Palace Avenue and Winner Street in premises once occupied by Evans, The Saddlers. It later opened a chemist shop adjoining. In 1920 it built a completely new and fully mechanised bakery. A foundation stone commemorates the opening. (The author's father's name appears on this as a member of the committee).

All these businesses were affected by the Second World War and other than the main store the other shops were closed down. The Society was eventually taken over by The Plymouth & South Devon Co-operative Society Limited and the corner shop, once occupied by Osbornes, together with adjoining properties was completely rebuilt.

The other large development was Dellers Stores. A sign above the shop in Winner Street claimed that it was established in 1844. A photograph taken about 1880 shows the original premises with a paraffin wagon outside. The business was acquired by Mr W. Lambshead who opened a large grocery and provision store in a new building on the north side of Palace Avenue, and subsequently a chemists shop adjoining. It is strange that Mr Lambshead always traded under the name of Dellers in all his developments. In 1936 he sold his premises to Chard Bros., who continued to run both the main premises in Palace Avenue and its branches. Dellers also established a chemist and opticians business (subsequently A.R.Baker) in the row of shops in Queens Park Mansions and a small tea shop and confectioners at the end of the block.

In about 1946 Chard Bros. sold the premises in Palace Avenue to the Rossiter family who purchased adjoining premises and expanded to become the large departmental store it is today. The adjoining chemist shop has continued as a separate private undertaking.

The development of Palace Avenue, Victoria Street and Torbay Road provided opportunity for the opening of many new retail businesses. Originally there were no shops on the north side of Palace Avenue Gardens and only a few on the South side, these included Axworthy's Printers & Stationers, The Paignton Observer office and later Milward Maxey's cycle and electrical shop and "Peters", tobacconist and men's hairdresser.

East of the Gardens, and in the same block as Dellers, were Lorimer (Ladies Outfitter), Weltons (Boots & Shoes), Pughs and Fred Sarson (Chemist). Sarsons is the only business still operating.

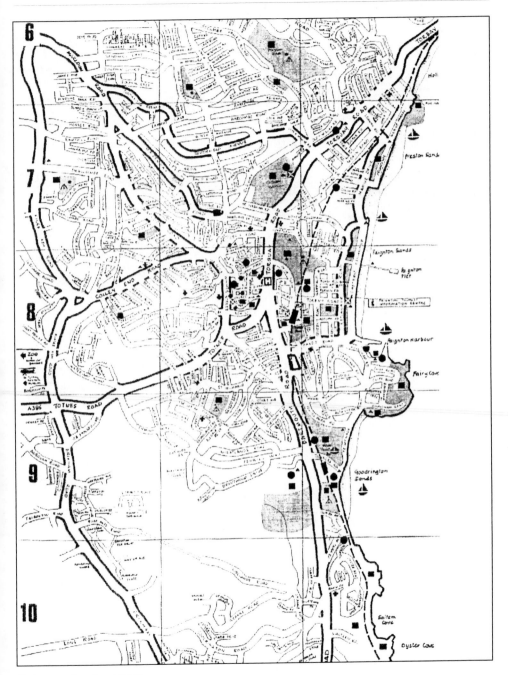

Paignton in the 1970's

Reproduced by kind permission of Ordnance Survey © Crown Copyright NC/2004/26031

The opposite side of the street has seen many changes. One of the earliest shops was that of Heaviside Piano Shop which was established in 1889. Another long established business was Church's China Shop which closed within the last few years. Other businesses which have come and gone are Hicks Palace Avenue Dairy, The Cash Tailoring Co. (subsequently Thorns), Ellis & Son, Ironmongers, Paignton Gas & Light Co. showroom and office. Practically the whole of this side is now occupied by banks.

Victoria Street was an invitation to the establishment of many businesses. It became a mixture of small locally owned shops and national companies. Only two of the early traders remain today i.e. Boots and W.H. Smith although Boots have moved from one side of the street to the other.

Two early shops were those on the corners with Victoria Square, i.e. The Maypole Dairy Company and The Penny Bazaar and Foale's the butcher. Emmanuel Beare opened his Ladies Shop in premises built in 1890 as a sign in a pediment at the top of the building confirms. The premises were taken over by Liptons in about 1950.

Among the early local shopkeepers were A. H. Braund, Milliner and Ladies Wear, Hunter Joy, Jewellers, Mortimer Ricks, Jeweller, Pascoe's Tripe Shop, Hunter Pork Butcher, Waycotts which was then a furniture shop, Wilcocks (butcher), Eastman (butcher) and more recently Spry the outfitter and Stone, the tobacconist whose shelves were stocked with jars of a variety of tobaccos and shop windows with a variety of pipes. At one time Paish & Co had a large piano shop on the same side. Around the corner in Station Square was Garths, Ladies Hairdresser and The Victoria Drug Stores. At one time there were four national footwear shops in Victoria Street; Olivers, Lennards, Frisby's and Stead and Simpson, all are no longer there,

Timothy Whites, the Chemist, had premises on the north side for many years. Other shops which have come and gone are Hicks Dairy, Valleys Ice Cream & Confectionery, International Stores, Brocks Furniture Shop and many others for short periods.

In about 1930 Messrs Harris Osborne opened a music and gramophone record shop in Totnes Road, in part of The Triangle block. Here one could listen to the latest 78's in specially constructed booths before making a purchase.

F.W. Woolworth & Co. built their first store in Station Square in 1932 by demolishing part of the Gerston Hotel. In 1964 a major development took place involving the demolition of the greater part of the Gerston Hotel.

The main development in Torbay Road was the building of Queens Park Mansions which incorporated a row of shops. Apart from premises occupied by Dellers, "Iredales" opened a book shop and library, (subsequently taken over by Bastins) and adjoining there was a large shop occupied by The Irish Linen Co.

On the same side of the road, extending from Queens Road to the seafront was a row of private houses which were converted to shops at a much later date.

The opposite side of the road was the long established Nell Popes Railway Temperance Hotel and Café while lower down was Garfield Terrace which gradually became a row of shops occupied by small local businesses down to Garfield Road comprising; Trewins (Tobacconist & Hairdresser) Godfreys (Top Shop), Parnell (Greengrocer), Perrets (Tailors and Men's Outfitters), Evans (Bakers & Confectioners), Germans (Photographers), Stanbury (Fishmongers) and, below Garfield Road on the north side there were only five shops, but more houses were gradually converted into shops until by 1911 there were nine shops.

Andrews Grocery & Provision Store on the corner with Garfield Road was one of the original shops, but this was destroyed by fire in the mid 1980's.

Among other shops which later became established were Goss Mabin (Jeweller), The Card Shop & Post Office, Browns (Ladies Outfitter), Suttons (Printers & Stationers) and Langfords (Umbrellas).

The Ordnance Survey Map dated 1904 shows two Garden Nurseries had been established on the east side of Torquay Road, possibly to supply plants etc. to the new villas which had been erected in the Roundham area.

Treseders Nursery occupied a large area of land at Fernham which later gave way to the development of Kings Road and adjoining properties.

The other nursery was Victoria Nurseries occupying land at the rear of Hyde Road which was acquired by the Council in 1927 to form part of Victoria Park.

CHAPTER TWENTY FOUR

Inns, Hotels, Boarding Houses and Holiday Camps

BEFORE THE RAILWAY CAME THERE WERE several Inns which had been long established. They were the old coaching hostelries or as taverns for local fishermen. Also situated in many parts of the town were what were described in Robinson's Directory as "lodgings", many of these were in the Polsham area.

The most famous of the Inns was "The Crown and Anchor" in Church Street. It was originally sited to the west of the Crown and Anchor archway with a large room extending over the archway. This room was used by the Local Board of Health from 1863 until the new Town Hall was built in 1870 with a small break when the meetings were held at the Clerk's residence. Petty Sessions, or Magistrate's Court, was held in the Great Room of The Crown and Anchor Inn until it was transferred to the new Town Hall in 1870. In about 1890 the property was divided into two, halving the size of the main room. The building was demolished in about 1892.

Mr Hyde Dendy introduced the first hotels into Paignton by building the Gerston Hotel in Station Square in 1870 and later extending it towards the railway. He also built the Esplanade Hotel in 1883 by joining up two villas. The development of other seafront hotels is described in a previous chapter.

Mr Henry John Bailey built Baileys Hotel in 1894 in Station Square. It never seemed to flourish as a hotel and has had several uses since it was built.

Another early hotel built in the late 1800's was Moore's Hotel in Dartmouth Road. This changed its name to Brown's Hotel and later to The Commercial Hotel. It was destroyed by fire, and later replaced by a new building named The Coverdale Hotel.

Many of the larger villas in the Roundham, Goodrington and seafront areas have been adapted and extended to become hotels.

Two purpose built hotels have been built in Paignton since the original old hotels were opened, that is "The Ship" in Manor Road and "The Waterside" on the Dartmouth Road.

Smaller villas and large terrace houses near the seafront and Goodrington have become "boarding houses", catering for visitors, but without large public rooms.

Between the two World Wars many of the large industrial towns and cities closed their works and mills for a week. These became known as Wakes Week in the north and midlands and by such other names as "Swindon Week", "Wales Week" etc. This led to housewives in the terrace houses of Colley End and St Michaels "taking in visitors". The G.W.R. ran special excursion trains to bring hundreds of visitors to the Town on such occasions. It became quite a money earner to the local housewives who passed on letters to one another according to the rooms they had available.

Holiday Camps

The first holiday camp in Paignton was The Nest Holiday Camp constructed in 1925 on a triangular site between Kings Ash Road, Colley End Road and Foxhole Road. It comprised a group of wooden chalets. The site has since been developed for sheltered housing.

Waterside Camp on the Dartmouth Road, adjoining Saltern Road, was started by a group of local business men in the late 1920's. The camp came under new ownership in the 1930's when it was managed by Mr and Mrs Corney who lived in a detached house at the entrance to the site. This was more of a "camp site" in that it provided tented accommodation and mobile caravans. The camp was purchased by the Council in May 1939, but was closed in August 1939 on the outbreak of World War II. It was reopened again after the War and in 1952 main drainage was provided and many improvements carried out.

Several other holiday camps were established in the 1930's. These included Louville Camp on the Dartmouth Road at Waterside, South Devon Holiday Camp at Kings Ash Hill, Devon Coast Country Club and the Torbay Chalet Hotel. Most of these sites have now been developed for housing. One large camp still existing is the Beverley Holiday Park on the Goodrington Road.

CHAPTER TWENTY FIVE

Laundries

BEFORE THE INTRODUCTION OF LAUNDRIES and washing machines most houses had a "copper". This was a brick or stone structure built in the corner of the kitchen or scullery and against an outside wall and about 3 ft high. In to the top was built a cast iron bowl about 18" in diameter with a wooden lid. Below the bowl was a fire grate with an exterior chimney stack.. The "copper" was used on wash days, usually once a week, when the bowl was partially filled with soapy water, heated by the fire beneath. Soiled clothes and bed clothes (washing) were placed in the very hot water and stirred with a wooden stick. After a time the "washing" was transferred to large galvanised baths or tubs where it was soaked in changes of water until all soap was removed. Where tubs were used a "podger" was used to help the process. The "washing" was then put through the "mangle" a manually operated machine with two wooden rollers, which could be adjusted for space, and finally hung outside on lines to dry. Ironing, or pressing, was carried out using cast iron "irons" heated on the kitchen stove.

Some of the larger houses such as Primley House had special laundry rooms with "live in" accommodation for laundry maids.

With the advent of hotels and boarding houses laundering began to be carried out on a commercial basis.

In the early days this was carried out by domestic laundries. One such existed in an end terrace house at the top of St Mary's Hill. Here the two Miss Hodges ran a laundry staffed two or three times a week by local housewives. Laundry was delivered and subsequently collected by horse drawn carriers in large cane baskets. At that time (about 1914) there was an underdeveloped building site at the rear of the house and this was used as a drying ground on lines suspended between wooden poles.

With the spread of the use of gas and the advent of motor vehicles The Paignton Sanitary Laundry Co. Ltd. established a steam laundry in Totnes Road, just above Collingwood Road. Early photographs show a motor van and ladies in the laundry room using gas fired hand irons. Lettering on the side of the van states that the company also undertook carpet cleaning, dry cleaning and dyeing. Steam from the boilers operated a hooter which was sounded at 7.50 am and 5.00 pm. The works closed after the outbreak of World War II when it became an engineering works.

Another "steam laundry" was established at about the same period at the bottom of Coombe Road in Preston. This was known as The Vectis Steam Laundry. The laundry was later re-sited in Lower Polsham Road near the Polsham Arms but this was later closed down.

CHAPTER TWENTY SIX

Cider, Beer, Wine and Lemonade

Cider

At the turn of the 19th-20th centuries there appears to have been three main cider makers in Paignton, although the town had been famous for its cider many years before.

Henleys Cider works were situated in Southfield Road adjoining the Methodist Church. The sandstone building still exists today although it has had many uses since cider making closed in about 1918. The author has many memories of this old works, which in place of windows had openings with vertical wooden slats and no glass. Through these openings one could see a cart-horse going round and round hitched to a large circular "pound" in which the apples were crushed. Also visible was the cider press with its large wheel and vertical screw.

Robinson's Directory of 1851 records that a Mr Nicholas Prout Hunt lived at Crabb's Park. He is thought to be the founder of N.P. Hunt & son who produced cider at Crabbs Park until they were taken over by H. & G. Simonds of Reading in 1916. The works were subsequently taken over by Whiteway Co. in 1934 who produced cider spelled with a 'y' as Cyder. In 1935 Whiteways changed the name of the works to "Crabbs Park Winery".

Grape juice was imported in large stainless steel tankers and a variety of bottled wine was produced such as "Sanatogen Tonic Wine" and various fruit wines as sherries.

For over 50 years the works was managed by Mr 'Bob' Loates and for many years the chemist was Mr Alaister Macrae.

The third cider makers were the Churchward family at Yalberton. Their cider was much sought after and although production diminished, cider continued to be produced until very recently.

The success of the local cider production was no doubt due to the fact that the slopes around the town produced suitable apples in abundance.

A large proportion of the cider produced in the early years was exported on small sailing vessels from Paignton Harbour when for many years there was a large sandstone building on the south quay, known as the cider store.

The works closed in 1987 and the land developed for housing.

Beer

It is not known when Paignton brewery was established, but early photographs show that it was run by Messrs Starkey, Knight & Ford. The fact that the building included a public bar named "The Victoria" gives some indication of the date. It was situated between Princes Street and Well Street on what became known as Brewery Hill.

There was a large yard on the opposite side of the road, originally part of the old vicarage grounds, used as stables for the horses and sheds for the drays. The business was later acquired by the national firm of Whitbread's and later demolished to give way to a housing project.

Wine

Reference is made to wine, partly because it has always been thought that at some time wine was produced in the area of Winner Street which at one time was Wynerde Street or Wine Street. It has also been rumoured that at one time vines were grown against the walls of the terraced gardens at the bottom of Marldon Road.

Another clue to the wine story is that Arthur Waycott had a Wine & Spirit shop in Winner Street in the early part of the 1900's (later Carr & Quicks). Adjoining the shop was a wide passageway leading to a large sandstone building at the rear which could well have been a vinery in earlier years.

Reference is made earlier to wine production at Crabbs Park.

Lemonade

At one time there was a Paignton Mineral Water Company, but the name which will be remembered by old Paigntonians is Dawes Mineral Waters. Herbert Dawe set up a mineral water factory, producing fizzy lemonade, in the early 1900's in premises at the rear of the Curledge Street Girls School. The lemonade was sold in bottles with a constricted neck which contained a small glass ball which sealed the gaseous contents. It required a special wooden opener with a central peg to release the ball.

The business was carried on by the Dawes' family who extended the line of product to various cordials. The factory closed many years later and was developed as a building site.

CHAPTER TWENTY SEVEN

Building method and Materials

BUILDING METHODS

The building activity taking place in the 1890's must have been amazing, both in scope and the skills displayed. There were no proper roads and the whole area must have been a field of mud. All building materials had to be brought in by horse drawn carts and timber wagons. There was no steel scaffolding, no metal ladders, no power operated hoists or mechanical mixers for mortar etc.

Scaffolding consisted of larch or fir poles lashed together with ropes with timber putlogs built into the walls as they were erected and rough timber planks. Many of the labourers who erected the scaffolding were ex-seafarers who had a good knowledge of knots and lashings. The sight of all the scaffolding on both sides of the streets must have been amazing. Access to the higher scaffold platforms was by means of ladders. These were constructed from poles sawn down the middle and with wooden bar steps. To reach the higher levels some of the ladders had to be very long and heavy. The last of these, owned by Messrs C. & R. E. Drew, nicknamed "Big Tom", was raised in Victoria Street in about 1928-30 to reach the roof of one of the buildings.

All bricks and mortar had to be carried to upper levels in hods, or in some cases the bricks were thrown, by hand, from platform to platform.

Mortar was mixed on large wooden decks at ground level.

The lifting of heavy items was by pulleys and ropes.

At this time many tools were made by the workmen, especially joiners, while other heavier items were made by local blacksmiths.

A revolution in building construction came with the introduction of "hollow" walls. Previously all walls both stone and brick were solid, battened and lath and plastered on the inside. "Hollow" walls were introduced after about 1920 and consisted of a half brick ($4^{1}/2$ ") outer skin with a 2" cavity between that and the inner skin which could be of any thickness from $4^{1}/2$" upwards. The two

skins were tied together with metal ties, usually of galvanised iron, twisted in the middle to prevent the passage of moisture. This method of construction obviated the use of battening and lath and plaster.

Since the early 1930's a great change has taken place in building methods. We have seen the introduction of tubular scaffolding, mechanical hoists and mobile cranes, mechanical diggers, dumper trucks and earth moving machines, on site mortar and concrete mechanical mixers, pre-mix concrete delivered to site, compressors and pneumatic tools, electrically powered machines of all kinds including hand tools and the introduction of health and safety regulations.

No one has discovered how to lay bricks by machine!

BUILDING MATERIALS

Sand

For many years sand for building was obtained from the sand dunes along the sea shore. Sand was also taken from the beaches, but this was not good as it contained salt. The levelling and grassing of the "Greens" in the late 1860 put an end to the collecting of sand from the dunes.

In 1898 The Paignton Improvement Act prohibited the removal of sand from the foreshore.

When the use of sea-sand ended, building sand was obtained from the River Dart. Sand was dredged from the river and brought in barges to Galmpton Quay where it was collected by horse and cart. For many years this was carried on by Langmead Brothers, but seems to have ceased during World War II.

The sand dredged from the Dart contained many impurities such as shells and loam and had to be washed and screened.

When the supply of Dart sand ceased "pit sand" was obtained from sand pits at Aller on the outskirts of Newton Abbot and from Lee Moor on the edge of Dartmoor.

Mortar

Three types of mortar were used in building, cement mortar, lime mortar and gauged lime mortar. Cement was an expensive material in the early days as it had to be "imported" whereas lime was readily available locally. Cement mortar was a mixture of Portland Cement and sand, usually in the proportion of one of cement to three of sand by volume mixed on a "banker" and used within an hour. It was chiefly used for "pointing" to protect work built in lime mortar. Joints were raked out to a depth of $3/4$" and "pointed" with cement mortar.

One of the first jobs on the building sites was to dig two pits. One was about 3' square and 3' deep over which a portable wooden hut was placed to form the latrine. The other pit was the lime pit. This was a pit about 8' x 6' x 3' deep (or larger for large projects) with a wooden open top box fitted at one end with a grid and sluice outlet. Specifications demanded that lime for mortar shall be well burnt stone lime. Burnt limestone (calcium oxide) from lime kilns was brought on site and tipped into the box and water added. This caused a chemical reaction which produced a boiling semi liquid. This liquid was then drained off into the pit and became "putty lime" (calcium hydroxide) or slaked lime which was used for mortar for walling or plastering. Many lime kilns can be seen in the surrounding countryside, but most lime was obtained from the quarry and kiln at Galmpton Quay. Lime mortar was usually in the proportion of one part putty lime to three of sand. When used for the first coat of plaster long clean cow hair, well beaten and picked, was added to the mortar. When used to line chimney flues cow dung was added to the mortar.

Gauged lime mortar was used where a more durable mortar was required. Cement was added to the lime mortar mix. Slaked lime mixed with water and size was used as the decorative material "lime wash".

In the late 1890's early 1900 clay was mixed with the lime mortar.

During the early 1930's a local firm installed a mortar mill in Littlegate Road. This consisted of a large circular metal pan which was traversed by two mechanically driven large rollers and blades. Mortar was produced by mixing and grinding lime putty and ashes from the gas works. This produced what was known as "pug mortar" or "black mortar". It produced problems due to injurious chemicals contained in the ash.

WALLING STONES

Sandstone

It will be obvious to anyone walking around the town that all the old buildings are built with red sandstone. Generally this was what was known as "conglomerate red sandstone"; sandstone containing pebbles of limestone. These pebbles varied in size and can be seen in the old walls in Tower Road and in the old boundary walls in Roundham Road. Finer grades were used for the better buildings. All the sandstone was obtained from local quarries. These were situated at the following sites: Well Street (old Council yard), rear of terrace of houses in Colley End Road, rear of Quarry Terrace in Marldon Road, off Maidenway Road, the harbour end of Cliff Road, at rear of terrace houses in Roundham Road facing the harbour, the old gas holder site at Hollicombe, off Derrell Road at St Michaels. The most recent quarry to be worked is in Barcombe Road.

Large blocks of sandstone were used for the building of the harbour and the sea wall at Paignton.

Limestone

Local limestone was not used for building until about 1870. One of the oldest buildings to be built of limestone is what is now The United Reformed Church in Dartmouth Road. This is built in roughly squared stones. These stones were squared "on site" and this might have led to the establishment of a stone mason's yard adjoining which was run for many years by Mr Pollard and later by his stepsons Bob & Allan Cummings. The yard and works were demolished in a road improvement scheme.

Another limestone building is the old Town Hall in New Street and the adjoining properties in Totnes Road, built in about 1870. This is built as "fair faced random rubble pointed in snail creep". A look at the buildings will show what this means.

Random rubble limestone was later extensively used for boundary walls.

Most of the limestone was obtained from quarries at Yalberton and later at Churston and on the Dartmouth Road.

Limestone was later used as "dressings" in conjunction with sandstone or brickwork as in Palace Avenue and Victoria Street. This limestone was of a finer quality and is thought to have been obtained from Torquay quarries.

A fine example of limestone masonry is the plinth of Lloyds Bank on the Totnes Road elevation. This would have been described as ashlar in lime mortar in large stones squared on beds and joints, quarry or bunched faced and pointed in cement mortar. The piers are built with large stones "quarry or bunched faced" with 2" chisel draughted margins.

The sea walls at Preston and Goodrington are built with large blocks of limestone. It will be seen that the walling shows little sign of weathering after more than 100 years.

Stone Dressings

Stone for dressings was "imported" from Portland, Beer and Bath. It is probable that the first two were brought in by sailing ships. This type of stone was fine grained and could be sawn and rubbed to give an even surface. Their early use was to provide sharp straight angles around door and window openings in buildings built of sandstone, but they were later used on all types of buildings to provide carved and moulded embellishments.

Bricks

The development of Palace Avenue and Victoria Street marked a change in building construction from stonework to brickwork. It will be seen that nearly all the buildings in these streets and in other buildings of the period, are faced with cream coloured brickwork. This was due to the fact that Messrs Hexter Humpherson had started to manufacture these bricks at Kingsteignton from the white clay obtained from pits in the vicinity. These bricks were hard and durable and with a smooth, weather resisting, face.

A little later in the early 1900's hard red bricks were imported from Wellington in Somerset and can be seen in the old Liberal Club building at the junction of Dartmouth and Totnes Roads.

At one time there were three brickworks in Paignton; at Primley (on the site now occupied by Safeway); on the Brixham Road opposite Battersway Road junction (now wholesale supply store) and on the Brixham Road at Claylands (now a D.I.Y. store). The first two named operated from about early 1900's whilst the third works were opened in the mid 1900's.

All these works produced what were known as "common" bricks. These were too soft and absorbent to be used as "facings".

Following the closure of these works most common bricks were brought into the area by The London Brick Company. At one time bricks were brought into Paignton Harbour from Holland.

Concrete

Very little information is available as to when concrete came into general use in building. The basic ingredients of concrete are cement, sand and gravel. Cement was the material in short supply and was expensive. It is thought that concrete came into general use in foundations, floors etc. after World War I.

Cement became more readily available when a cement works was set up on the outskirts of Plymouth and reinforced concrete was in general use.

Timber

Timber was readily available at the time of the town centre expansion. Oak, elm and fir could be felled in nearby forests and fir, deal, etc. was being imported into Torquay by Crossmans and into Totnes by Reeves from the Baltic ports and North America.

ROOFING MATERIALS

Thatch

Prior to the coming of the railway most buildings had thatched roofs. Reeds being readily available from the local marshes. Some thatched roofs still exist today.

Slates

Slates followed thatch and a small quantity was brought into Paignton Harbour in the 1850's.

Practically all buildings erected in the late 1880's and early 1900's were roofed with slates. The majority were brought in by rail in truck loads from north and south Wales and smaller quantities from Cornwall.

A few years after World War I a clay roofing tile works was established on the outskirts of Exeter. The distinctive red tiles all bore the name "rougemont" impressed on the underside. It can be seen that most buildings erected from about 1920 are roofed with tiles.

For a short period asbestos "slates" were used and more recently concrete "tiles" have come into common use.

Lead

For years lead had been used for covering the "flat" roof areas of ecclesiastical buildings, castles and the like, but this was a very expensive form of roofing. It was followed by copper and zinc.

Other Materials

Corrugated iron sheets were used for commercial and agricultural buildings. For a time corrugated asbestos was used for factories, agricultural buildings and small domestic out-buildings, but asbestos was banned some years later as being injurious to health.

In the early 1920's a new roofing material "Ruberoid" was introduced on to the building materials market. It was a "rubberised" felt supplied in rolls. Its initial use was for flat roofs of outbuildings and the like laid in one or two layers secured with galvanised clout nails. From this developed "three layer bituminous flat roofing".

This revolutionised the use of "flat" roofs in building. The material became a bitumised felt and was laid in hot bitumen in three overlapping layers. Many specialist flat roofing firms were established. The felt came in rolls and the bitumen in large blocks which were melted down on site in large caldrons and spread from what looked like large watering cans. The general system has continued to this day, but with improved systems and cold bitumen sealer.

Damp Proof Courses

Most pre 1900 buildings had no damp proof course to prevent rising damp. In the late 1800's when slates became available damp proof courses were built into walls about 9" above ground level consisting of two courses of slates, laid to "break joint" in cement mor-

tar. Later, with the introduction of bitumen, damp proof courses consisted of rolls of bituminous felt laid on a mortar bed. In some cases the bituminous felt had a thin lead layer in the centre.

Glass

Many "acres" of glass must have been used in the rapid expansion of Palace Avenue, Victoria Street etc.

Glass was manufactured by Pilkington Brothers at St Helens, Lancashire and one wonders how it found its way to Paignton. One theory is that it was imported by sea into Plymouth by the firm Andrewartha and that it was subsequently transported by road.

Materials Generally

Since 1900 many improvements have taken in the manufacture and use of building materials, almost too numerous to mention. One of the major changes has been the substitution of copper and subsequently plastic, for internal plumbing also in decorative materials.

Slaked lime has given way to hydrated lime and gypsum plaster.

CHAPTER TWENTY-EIGHT

Paignton Zoo

IT SEEMS FITTING TO END THIS BOOK WITH A chapter beginning with "Z". It is also the shortest chapter because it would be presumptuous to improve on what has already been written by the late Jack Baker in his book entitled "Chimps, Champs and Elephants".

Paignton Zoo is undoubtedly one of the main tourist attractions to have been established since the railway came.

(Copies of Jack's book may be obtained at the Zoo or through local bookshops).

Epilogue

"There was a time when Paignton was a marvellous town to live in.
But when?"